When I Was Saddam's Hostage

By

Ali R. Bozkurt

AuthorHouse™
1663 Liberty Drive
Bloomington, IN 47403
www.authorhouse.com
Phone: 1 (800) 839-8640

Published by AuthorHouse 12/21/2018

ISBN: 978-1-4107-8604-3 (sc)
ISBN: 978-1-4107-8603-6 (e)

Library of Congress Control Number: 2003097525

Print information available on the last page.

Table of Contents

CRISIS IN THE GULF: IRAQ'S INVASION OF KUWAIT

Turk Released From Baghdad Detention Center Tells Grim Story

By Thomas Goltz
Special to The Washington Post

ANKARA, Turkey, Aug. 17—A Turkish contractor who was captured by Iraqi troops in Kuwait and detained in a Baghdad detention center returned to Ankara this week and painted a bleak portrait of the treatment of some foreign hostages in Iraq.

"It was unbelievable," said Ali Riza Bozkurt, president of the contracting firm Birlesmis Muhendis Burosu. It was "worse than what . . . concentration camps [appear] to be in the movies. There was one working toilet for 1,000 people, with scum running over your heels when you went in."

At the time of Iraq's Aug. 2 invasion, Bozkurt and 30 of his project engineers were in Kuwait to test a housing complex for Turkish workers helping to construct the $350 million Subiyah thermal power plant. The facility was being built by the emir of Kuwait as the key installation of a projected $30 billion satellite city, in part to underline the Kuwaiti government's claim to land along the country's northern border.

While working that day, Bozkurt said in an interview after returning to Ankara on Tuesday, he spotted thousands of troops and tanks moving south.

"We didn't know who it was at first," Bozkurt said. "Then I called the undersecretary of energy [of Kuwait] who was due at the job site and explained the situation to him, and he went into shock. The Iraqis were already 150 miles inside Kuwait territory and the government had no idea."

The Turkish team holed up in their quarters, which quickly came under Iraqi military guard, he said. Iraqi troops began streaming into the area, many of them in search of water.

"They had been without water for eight hours and were crazed," Bozkurt said. "After they overran the camp, some of the Iraqis started tearing apart the sewage pipes under our villas just to moisten their lips, even with raw sewage."

Over the next few days, Bozkurt said he and his engineers were transported north toward the Iraqi city of Basra, traveling through several dozen military encampments.

"It was like a tour for a spy or something—we saw everything. And with our own experience in the army, coupled with our training as draftsmen, we even drew comprehensive maps of all the Iraqi fortifications, most of which were designed to resist attack from the sea," he said.

The Turks were force to spend the first two nights in the desert until an Iraqi military official in Basra took control of the group. The official, according to Bozkurt, apologized for the poor treatment of the Turks and assured them that they would be released once they reached Baghdad.

A train was commandeered, Bozkurt said, and his group went aboard, along with more than 1,000 other foreigners in the custody of Iraqi troops, including workers from the Philippines, South Korea and Turkey, soldiers, policemen and officials from Kuwait, and Saudi nationals who had been taken from their luxury hotel beds in Kuwait City.

"We thought it was over—clean sheets, excellent food and fruit—with the commander apologizing to us repeatedly," Bozkurt said. The festive atmosphere aboard the train lasted until Baghdad, when the group was placed on a convoy of 20 buses and driven around Baghdad.

"We thought they were going to drop us at our respective embassies as promised," Bozkurt said, "so we all waved back at the crowds. Pictures of [Iraqi President] Saddam Hussein were everywhere. It seemed like an entire nation of Saddams."

But the tour ended at the gates of a camp that apparently had been designed to hold prisoners captured in the eight-year war with Iran, which ended in 1988.

Bozkurt said he and the others on the buses were forced into two barrack-like structures, each housing 700 people. A third, smaller structure, Bozkurt said he learned, housed about 30 Westerners who had been taken from Kuwait by Iraqi troops and brought to Baghdad.

"For some reason, the Iraqis had already divided the Westerners they had taken from the Kuwait Sheraton into two groups," he said. "They had removed the Americans, Britons, Germans, Spanish and Italians to different quarters, and we never saw them. But the remaining group contained everyone from a Russian diplomat to a Japanese billionaire, four Hungarian telephone technicians and three Greek sailors from a ship docked in Basra."

According to Bozkurt, the accommodations in the Baghdad camp were dismal. "It was strange, seeing captains of industry and men who only stayed in luxury hotels reduced to sleeping on blankets and eating from a communal pot of soup with no spoons and eating bread that could be used in constructing a wall," he said.

A Japanese man who told fellow hostages that he was the president of a $3 billion-a-year Osaka-based corporation was "in a near state of shock," Bozkurt said. "So were many of the Saudis."

Bozkurt said he maintained calm and even devised an escape plan—never used—along with his fellow Turkish engineers. He said he managed to keep a hand-held tape recorder, making notes until he ran out of batteries. He compiled a list of the names and contact addresses for 1,630 prisoners in his camp. The prisoners also devised a makeshift refrigerator from a closed container given to the group and some wiring, he said.

On Aug. 11, Bozkurt said, he and the rest of the Turks, along with all Iranian, Afghan and Chinese nationals from the camp, were released. After recuperating for one night in a luxury hotel on the Tigris, they were taken by bus to Jordan, and Bozkurt continued home to Turkey.

"When we left, we saw, with our own eyes, four other camps just like ours—4,000 people," he said.

Introduction

They approached our construction site in the northern Kuwaiti desert driven by thirst. Their lips were chapped and peeling, their uniforms torn and stained, their boots split open and laces broken, their faces turning purple in the searing heat. At first there were only a few, then dozens, then hundreds of Iraqi soldiers, begging us for water, telling us they had been marching all day with nothing to drink. They were part of the Iraqi forces that had invaded Kuwait on that infamous day, August 2, 1990. My colleagues and I were amazed at how weakened and desperate they were, and wondered what type of regime would treat its own soldiers so badly. But we would soon find out, for we were about to become captives of their boss, Saddam Hussein, to be taken into Iraq, and to be paraded in the streets of Baghdad and imprisoned as pawns in a high-stakes global game that would leave its mark on us forever.

It was not what we had planned. Turkish and Kuwaiti officials had assured us that Saddam Hussein had been only rattling his sabers - that there was little reason to believe he would actually carry out his threats to seize Kuwait. The long awaited opening ceremony at the construction site therefore would be held as planned. I was chairman of the Turkish construction firm contracted by Kuwait to build the massive power station at Sabiya, 120 kilometers north of Kuwait City and 150 kilometers from the border with Iraq. The construction facilities had been completed and the scheduled event was to mark the beginning of work on the power station itself. The guest of honor would be the Undersecretary of Kuwait's Ministry of Electricity and Water. It was to be a very big day for our firm. But it turned out to be a dark day for the world. The repercussions continue to be enormous.

Inside of a few hours, all our work and planning on the project seemed to matter less and less. The long and difficult bidding process and the complex logistics involved in desert construction receded from focus as the reality of our captivity set in. There were thirty-two of us - myself, nine of our firm's top engineers and managers, and twenty-two construction workers, all of us Turks. We were taken by force and jailed in Iraq, jammed into a concentration camp with at least a thousand other prisoners of many nationalities who had also been abducted from Kuwait.

Many things that we had taken for granted in our lives were suddenly gone, but nothing so much as our freedom. Our fear was compounded by the constant uncertainty, never knowing what Saddam Hussein had in mind for us, but being well aware that he would not think twice about executing us if it served his interests. Then there was the isolation, being cut off from the rest of the world except for the broadcasts of a small transistor radio that we had smuggled past our captors. The news that came to us through this tenuous link often raised more questions than it answered - Would Iraq be invaded? Would we be bombed? Should we try to escape? - and at times seemed to increase our feeling of abandonment. There was no way of contacting our families, no way of knowing whether anyone "out there" knew what had happened to us. That was why we carved our names on the walls of the prisons where they put us, so that if we did not make it out alive, if someday we just disappeared, there would at least be some trace of our having been there, some evidence that we were more than simply "missing."

For the same reason, I kept a journal nearly every step of the way, in the hope that our story would become known no matter how it ended. And in a deeper sense, the mere act of recording our life inside the dictator's labyrinth was itself an act of defiance against the isolation he had imposed on us.

The story I am going to tell in these pages is about survival, survival in the face of repression, and about holding on when the world seems to be coming apart. It's about a group of people trying to keep their wits and their sense of humor, leaning on the best of human nature and trying to fend off the worst, and working to cooperate for the sake of everyone even as the circumstances become increasingly more difficult.

In the end, we were fortunate. For many others who have been caught up in the web of Iraq, and especially for the Iraqis themselves, it has been much worse, often deadly. But our experience of overcoming imprisonment and fear, and bridging differences of language and culture along the way, is one that I hope can inspire. Not that I would wish on anyone what we went through on anyone. But if our experience can in any way bring about a stronger appreciation for human freedom, and perhaps energize others to work on behalf of those who still do not enjoy it, then it's a story worth telling.

Wednesday, August 1st, 1990

The offices of Turkish Joint Venture (TJV) in downtown Kuwait City were busier than usual - computer networks humming, design meetings underway, subcontractors being contacted and purchasing orders being completed. The ceremonial opening of the work at the Sabiya power plant was scheduled for the next morning at 9 am and the entire staff was energized. It would be the culmination of a great amount of work and preparation, and the beginning of one of the biggest construction projects in the Persian Gulf in nearly twenty years.

As Chairman of TJV, I was very proud of our efforts. Four Turkish companies had come together to form TJV, including my own BMB United Engineers Group. The other members of the partnership were SOYUT, SOYTEK and YAPI MERKEZI. My partners elected me Chairman. In 1989 TJV had entered a bid of $356 million to become the contractor for the Sabiya project, in competition against some 120 firms from twenty different nations. Following long and difficult negotiations TJV was selected and we signed a contract with the Kuwaiti government to construct the power station in five years, employing up to five thousand workers. We were proud not just for ourselves, but also for Turkey. Moreover, we knew that if this project went well, we could capitalize on the expected boom in the region in the wake of the war between Iraq and Iran.

1

Previously, I had been chairman of the BIMHOL construction company, which had successfully completed a number of jobs in Saudi Arabia, including tunnel projects in Mecca and housing projects in Medina. BIMHOL had been the first Turkish construction outfit to operate abroad. As these projects were being completed, however, the conflict between Iraq and Iran broke out, which caused a decline in construction throughout the Gulf. I took the opportunity to move to America, to secure higher education for my three daughters, and to carry out a number of research endeavors related to my profession at various U.S. universities and technical institutions, in continuation of my studies at the Istanbul Technical University where I had received a degree in civil engineering in 1963.

The war finally drew to a close in 1988. New construction possibilities were opening up and I returned to the Gulf to continue what had already become nearly two decades in overseas contracting. The experience of our company in Saudi Arabia during the 1970s, and in Kuwait as well, helped tremendously in winning the contract for the Sabiya plant. And, as a youth forty years ago, I had spent a good amount of time camping in the valleys of the Soguk Pinar of Sivas, called the "Mamas," and I thought the experience might be helpful when it came to adapting to the rugged life ahead in Sabiya. Little did I know how much more rugged things would become, and in less than twenty-four hours.

We had built our construction site at Sabiya during six months of nearly non-stop work - the administration buildings, the pipelines, living quarters for thousands of workers, the storage areas, the laboratories that would be utilized for quality assurance testing, and all the other facilities needed to make this project go. Much of the heavy machinery - hundreds of pieces of equipment - had already been brought onto the site and the excavation had begun. A steady stream of trucks and tractor trailers poured daily onto the site, delivering all manner of materials, such as steel sheeting, structural steel and rebar. The main water pipeline had been connected to the Kuwait City system. The permits for the Turkish workers had been completed and hundreds of them had already arrived in Kuwait.

We also had received final approval from the Alahli Bank, one of the principal institutions contributing to the financing of the project. And now the Ministry of Electricity and Water had informed us that the Undersecretary himself, Mr. Abdullah Al-Minayes, and his deputy, Mr. Al-Enizi, wanted personally to be present for the start of the next stage of the project and to review the work schedule.

We were more than a year ahead of schedule and ready to keep up the pace to build the power station a year and a half ahead of our contractual deadline. We were confident that the Undersecretary would approve our timetable. The next day would not only mark the formal inauguration of this project; it would herald what everyone at TJV hoped would be a long and productive future for the firm, not only in Kuwait but with further projects throughout the region.

To ensure that all went well the following morning, I planned for me and our top engineers and managers, as well as a number of our construction foremen and workers, to travel to the site the night before, to ensure that all was in order prior to the Undersecretary's arrival. The main body of the work crew would follow early the next day.

That evening I passed through our offices, where everyone seemed to be in a controlled rush, to complete the last minute preparations. Department heads were barking orders and trying to complete reports, while aides and secretaries were darting from room to room trying to keep up.

I spent a few moments with Osman Mimarsinanoglu, the TJV project manager for Sabiya. He and I had been working

3

closely for twenty years and were close friends. He held a degree in civil engineering, earned in 1966 at the Middle East Technical University (ODTU), one of the best in Turkey. He had been the general manager of most of my companies and a partner in all of them, including BIMHOL in Saudi Arabia. As one of the most experienced and talented engineers in Turkey, he was the obvious choice to oversee the power station project in Kuwait.

I reminded Osman that no matter how late they had to work, he and the assistant project managers, the department heads and the selected group of construction workers were to travel to the Sabiya site that night. After a final look around the office, I found my driver, an Indian man named Thomas, and we began the journey north. The late model Lincoln was equipped with a mobile telephone, computer and copier machine, which allowed me to use the car as an office during long trips.

But I did not work in the car that night. Nor did I chat with Thomas, as I often liked to do, or listen to the radio. Instead I found myself going over the project in my head, vaguely aware of the quiet murmur of the Lincoln as it sped out of Kuwait City. I thought of the site at Sabiya, and the 150 kilometers of emptiness between it and Iraq. Some people in Kuwait were worried by the recent deployment of Iraqi troops near the border and the threatening language coming from Baghdad. But Kuwaiti officials did not seem particularly concerned.

Still, I had sought the view of the Turkish ambassador in Kuwait City, Mr. Guner Oztek. He told me there should not be anything to worry about, that Iraq was acting impetuously, but that it was just a bluff. No government in the region or elsewhere supported the idea of an invasion and sooner or later Saddam Hussein would have to back down. I had always respected Mr. Oztek's views. I had asked for and benefited from his counsel on a number of previous occasions, even when I had been initially skeptical of his advice. So I found his belief that there was no actual threat reassuring and my thoughts returned to the project.

After a drive of an hour and a half or so, we arrived at the site. Surrounded by desert, but less than two miles from the Gulf, it seemed serene beneath a vibrant night sky. I was met by three of our top people on the Sabiya project who had arrived earlier in the day.

Ibrahim Mender, a well-built man in his forties with curly gray hair, had overseen, as the chief electrical engineer, the construction of all the offices and buildings at Sabiya.

Ozer Ozkan, who was in charge of all our surveying and topographical work, was a slightly round, fatherly man who, although in his fifties, was among the most energetic of our group.

And Sedat Yildirim, a retired colonel in the Turkish military, was our site manager, overseeing everything from personnel to the giant kitchen built to feed a thousand workers at a time. In his mid-forties and in excellent physical shape, he had managed construction camps in a number of countries, under all kinds of conditions, and was one of the best in his field.

By the time they had briefed me on the preparation for the morning's activities, it was approaching midnight and I said we should get some sleep and meet with our entire team at seven the next morning for a final review.

Thursday, August 2nd, 1990

I awoke and looked at my watch. It read 6:30 am. For a few moments I was not sure where I was or why I was in this unfamiliar room. Early morning light filtered through the window across from me. The air-conditioner in the window above the bed was making a strange sound. It seemed to be straining against the immense desert heat that was already beginning to bake Sabiya. I remembered that the forecast was for 50 degrees Centigrade by midday - and that would be in the shade.

There was a knock at the door. It was Osman, his large frame leaning into the room. He said that Iraq had invaded Kuwait. I was not amused and asked him if he had any better jokes for that hour of the morning. But then I saw the genuinely concerned expression on his face and realized he was not kidding. Osman is very easy going, typical of a man from Anatolia in the Kayseri region of southern Turkey, and if Osman was anxious about something then you knew the situation was serious.

He said that Mehmet, one of our drivers, had just arrived alone from Kuwait City. He was supposed to have been leading a caravan of buses carrying four hundred construction workers to the site in time for the ceremony. But they were stopped by Kuwaiti police who said they could not go any further because Iraqi forces had penetrated Kuwait from the north. Eventually, he had persuaded the police to let him proceed so that he could retrieve the engineers and construction workers already at the Sabiya site.

Osman said that everyone who had arrived the night before was gathering outside and that what sounded like artillery fire could be heard in the distance. Just at that moment there was a deep, muffled roar, as if an underground excavation blast had been set off, shaking the floor and walls of the portable sleeping cabin. I told Osman I would meet everyone for breakfast in a few minutes. I took a quick shower, dressed in the green, light-cotton outfit I had acquired specifically for the day's activities, and laced up the sturdy, boot-like shoes I preferred to wear when working onsite.

I left the cabin and went over to the cafeteria complex. Inside I ran into Osman and two other members of our engineering teem, Husnu Tozeren and Mehmet Cetinkoprulu, both of them assistant project managers, and a number of the construction workers. All of them were asking me what we were going to do.

Husnu, who like Osman had received his engineering degree from ODTU, was known for his sharp, analytical mind and ability to remain calm under pressure, assets, I had a feeling, that would become increasingly valuable as I listened to another round of ominous explosions in the distance.

Mehmet Cetinkoprulu was our chief construction overseer for the Sabiya project. Handsome with chiseled features and just forty years old, he already had a number of years' experience running construction projects for the Kutlutas company, including projects in Baghdad. His particular specialty was power plants.

I told everyone to sit back down to their breakfasts and joined them. Husnu, Mehmet and the construction workers at neighboring tables tried to make a show of eating as normal. But with each new round of explosions, some of which seemed to be getting closer, knives and forks would stop in midair and bodies would shudder.

We hoped that the artillery fire, if that was what the explosions were, meant that the Kuwaiti army was trying to counter the Iraqi forces. Even so, it was hard to imagine that the Iraqis could have penetrated 150 kilometers into Kuwait in such a short time.

The construction workers listened intently as the other engineers and I tried to assess the situation. Osman pointed out that Sabiya was on a peninsula just across from Bubiyan Island in the Gulf. Our construction site was actually quite close to the bridge that connected the island to the mainland. One of Iraq's demands of Kuwait was that it hand over Bubiyan so that Iraq could have clear access to the Gulf. Osman said he was afraid that the Iraqis had gone crazy and were trying to seize Bubiyan by force. If so, we were going to be in the middle of a crossfire.

We also considered that Iraq's territorial claims on Kuwait dated back generations. There was an ancient arch called the Gate of Baghdad in downtown Kuwait City and Saddam Hussein's regime claimed that it marked what was the true southern border of Iraq. The Gate was right next to the Sheraton Hotel. Kuwaitis generally joked about Iraq's claim, as did foreign guests at the Sheraton when told the meaning of the gate.

Then there was the issue of the Rumaila oil field. Spanning southern Iraq and a small part of northern Kuwait, it was one the richest in the world. But because of geological configurations below the surface, the oil deposits were proportionately greater on the Kuwaiti side, much to the frustration and envy of Iraq.

There was also the question of Iraq's debt to Kuwait. Kuwait, along with Saudi Arabia and the United Arab Emirates, had given Iraq enormous amounts of aid during the war with Iran. Iraq owed Kuwait alone between thirty and forty billion U.S. dollars, a substantial drag on Iraq's plans for rebuilding following the war. There was therefore speculation that Saddam Hussein was threatening to invade partly to pressure Kuwait to forgive the debt.

Recently, Iraq had stepped up its demands and Kuwait had agreed to a number of official and multilateral regional meetings to discuss them. One meeting had taken place in Saudi Arabia in the city of Jeddah, where Saudi Arabia and a number of other Arab nations had attempted to mediate, but without much success. Reports soon followed of an Iraqi military build-up along the border with Kuwait.

Still, there had been a general sense that diplomatic pressure, particularly from the Arab world and from America, which had also backed Iraq against Iran, would keep Saddam Hussein from pulling the trigger against Kuwait. This was part of the reason why Mr. Oztek, the Turkish ambassador in Kuwait, had been confident there would be no invasion.

Our attempt to assess the situation was interrupted when Ibrahim and Ozer rushed into the cafeteria, wide-eyed and breathless. They had just come from another part of the construction site, a fenced-in area encompassing the storage places, laboratories, administrative offices and offices of the Kuwait Ministry of Electricity and Water. Because of the way the construction site was spread out across the desert, the area was about two kilometers away from the cafeteria and the sleeping units.

Ibrahim and Ozer said that when they had been returning, bombs had fallen around them and an artillery shell of some sort had whistled over their heads and exploded in their path. They said they had also seen tanks and soldiers maneuvering near the walled perimeter of the site. We assumed they were Kuwaiti army units, possibly there to defend the site, and speculated that a few of their artillery rounds had gone astray. Some of the engineers urged that we leave the site immediately and return to Kuwait City.

I called the Kuwaiti Ministry and managed to reach the Undersecretary's deputy, Mr. Al-Enizi. I told him about the situation at the site, and asked what the Undersecretary's plans were. Mr. Al-Enizi, who sounded somewhat distracted, said that under the circumstances he did not think that his boss would be coming to the site today.

I then tried to telephone the Turkish embassy in Kuwait City, but all the lines were busy. I thought it might be a problem with my cellular telephone so I drove to the administration office to use the portable telephone there. I heard a new series of explosions and could feel the concussions as they rippled through the interior of the vehicle. At the office I discovered that Ozer, in his haste, had taken the portable with him. That left me with the mobile phone in the Lincoln. As I was driving back to the living area of the camp, I was simultaneously dialing the embassy, again without success, and using my hand-held recorder to tape the sound of the ongoing explosions.

I decided it was time to get back to Kuwait City. We put the engineers into three jeeps and the construction workers onto the bus that the driver, Mehmet, had arrived in that morning. Two of the Turkish security guards for the site volunteered to stay behind, one of them from Karadeniz in northern Turkey and the other from Anatolia, where Osman was from. As the rest of the team departed, Ozer, Ibrahim and I spent about ten minutes briefing the volunteers on how to use the telephone and what numbers to call to reach us.

At that point, military aircraft started flying over the site and we feared we were about to be attacked from the air. The site was the only major installation of any sort in the northern sector of Kuwait and, because of the walled-in layout, could easily have been mistaken for a military base from overhead. Each time one of the planes roared overhead, we would involuntarily hunch our shoulders and duck. Fearing for the safety of the two security guards, we decided to take them back with us after all.

That meant there were six of us: the two volunteers, Mehmet Aktas and Mehmet Turgut, Ozer Ozkan, Ibrahim Mender, my driver, Thomas, and myself. Thomas and I went in the Lincoln and the rest in a Pajero jeep. I decided to make one last stop at the administration offices before leaving.

As we circled past the desert on the site's main road, I spotted some tanks down near the shore by the Gulf, maybe five hundred meters away. Then, coming in the other direction, I saw a car belonging to the Ministry of Electricity and Water. It must have been coming from the guard house manned by the Ministry at the entrance to the construction site. The car stopped and inside the vehicle were the two security guards who were stationed their permanently, both of them Egyptian, one of them quite overweight. They told us we should return to Kuwait City immediately.

Just then, one of the tanks by the shoreline opened fire. This was followed by the firing of automatic weapons. We scrapped our plan to stop at the office and drove rapidly toward the intersection of the main road to the city, which was also the only paved road between Iraq and Kuwait. Our pulses were racing. We had heard stories about combat and seen footage of it on television, but nothing had prepared us for the sensation of being in the middle of it.

As we sped along, tanks, armored cars and troops began to appear along the roadside. Somehow, I got through finally on my mobile phone to Ambassador Oztek in Kuwait City. My watch said 8:41 am, a little more than three hours since I had awakened. Reflexively, I waved at the soldiers marching along the roadside. Many of them waved back.

I told Ambassador Oztek that the entire TJV crew had just left the construction site and that we were on our way to Kuwait City. I described to him all the soldiers and military hardware we were passing on the road and he asked whether they were Kuwaiti or Iraqi. I said I couldn't really tell but I thought they were Kuwaitis - I didn't see how the Iraqis could already be so far south. Plus, they were letting us drive right on through.

As we got closer to the main road, I could see another group of tanks coming from the other direction. Eventually it combined with the units we were passing to create a massive formation.

I called the Ministry and again got Mr. Al-Enizi on the line. He asked me the same question: whose army was it? I told him the same thing, that I thought they were Kuwaitis, but that we were coming to the main highway and I would get out and make sure. How, I asked myself, could the Iraqi army be more than halfway to Kuwait City and the Kuwaiti government not even know about it?

At the intersection, hundreds of armored vehicles were lined up, each one carrying two or three dozen soldiers. I told Mr. Al-Enizi to hold on and stepped out of the Lincoln with the phone pressed to my ear. The soldiers atop the nearest armored vehicle looked at me, first with curiosity, then with confusion. Later, I would find out that the uniforms of high-ranking Iraqi military officers, especially generals, were similar to the green outfit I was wearing and that they often traveled in late-model luxury vehicles.

So, it could have been that we had been allowed to travel as far as we had because the soldiers thought I was one of their commanders. In any event, when I asked these soldiers whether they were Kuwaiti or Iraqi, they started yelling wildly, "Kuwait harabat, Kuwait harabat, Iraqi, Iraqi" - "Kuwait has been destroyed, we are Iraqis!"

Just as I was saying into the telephone, "Oh Lord, they are Iraqis," one of the soldiers ran at me and lunged. Then an officer confronted me. I told him it was my personal telephone, but he ordered me to hand it over immediately. Still too stunned to register the danger we were in, I held it away from him. Then Thomas started yelling at the soldiers, demanding that they leave me alone - but to no avail; they grabbed me and pulled the phone from my grasp. They demanded to know if there were other phones and I said no. They searched my small carrying case and found my tape recorder. They hit the play button and heard some of my business related dictation from days past. They played around with it some more and, possibly because they were satisfied that it could not be used for communication, handed it back to me.

I saw the minibus and the jeeps with the other engineers and our construction workers coming back in our direction. They stopped at the intersection and Thomas pulled the Lincoln alongside. Iraqi military convoys - armored cars, jeeps, tanks, troop carriers - were swarming all around us, some heading south, others toward the shoreline and others toward our construction site. I had never seen such a massive military display; none of us had. As the vehicles thundered past, engines roaring, metal clanging, I felt a knot begin to tighten in the center of my chest.

Another Iraqi officer ran up and shouted to us in halting English to return to wherever we had come, immediately. He said that Kuwait City had been destroyed and it was not possible to go there.

So we drove back toward the site, the rumble of explosions and the sharp report of automatic weapons getting louder as we got closer to the shoreline. The ground shook and I could feel the heat of war upon me. I was afraid for my life; and so was everyone in the group.

Our little convoy became separated and only some of the vehicles arrived with us back in the living area. Sedat, our site manager, asked if we could talk in his office. He said that because of the uncertainty of the situation we needed to formulate an emergency plan and offered his suggestions.

After about ten minutes we agreed on what had to be done. We then tried to gather everyone in the cafeteria. Osman and the other engineers who had lagged behind finally arrived and we were all together again. By now it was midmorning and we could feel the rising temperature whenever the door to the cafeteria was opened.

I started by saying that we needed to be prepared for every contingency, and that if anything happened to me, Osman would be in charge, followed by Sedat.

Having taken an inventory of our provisions, we informed everyone that thanks to the preparations for the day's inauguration ceremony, the camp was fairly well stocked. The water towers in the different sectors of the site were nearly full and there was enough food for five hundred people for a week. Meanwhile, the site was protected by relatively high concrete walls and sandbags, which was comforting - unless the Iraqis decided it would make a good military base.

Sedat explained the various measures to be taken. One was to give each of us a list of all our names and addresses so that if anyone managed to get out, they would be able to provide information about the others. We would also hang white sheets from the eight-meter water tanks, to indicate to the Iraqis that the site was not a military installation.

Next, we would park the vehicles in different locations, spread all around the site. This would mean that if there was an artillery or aerial attack, they would not be as easily destroyed as they would if they were parked together.

The main problem, for which there was no real solution, was that we had no way to communicate with anyone outside the site. My mobile telephone was gone. The only other one had been with Ozer and Ibrahim in the Pajero jeep. But they had been caught off guard too, and had left it lying on the back seat where the soldiers who had stopped them had seen it and snatched it away.

The meeting ended and some of us began writing the lists of names and addresses. Others found poles and rigging to hang the white sheets from the water towers like flags, and then repositioned the vehicles. Some of the engineers tried to lighten the atmosphere, joking about what it would have been like to show the Undersecretary around while the explosions were going off. Some of the construction workers climbed the water tanks, hoping to get a better view of what was happening. We warned them against exposing themselves like that. But when they came down, others went up; their curiosity getting the better of them.

It was nearly noon and Sedat had prepared lunch as though it were any other day. As we were discussing whether there were any other contingencies we should consider, there was an enormous explosion and our plates nearly jumped off the table. We ran outside and saw fire and black smoke billowing from the Kuwaiti border police station. It made me think of the nearby Kuwaiti radar installation, another probable target. We were clearly in the line of fire. And what if the Iraqi forces saw some connection between the radar and our construction site? Would they disregard the white sheets and fire on us anyway?

We went back inside the cafeteria and tried to stay calm. Some of the group brought out a deck of cards, while others talked quietly among themselves. Then one of construction workers poked his head round the door and said he had a radio, whereby we all ran outside to see what he was talking about. It was a small, old transistor model. Its antenna had seen better days and there was some static, but it still functioned quite well. When the twelve o'clock news came on, the lead story was Kuwait's collapse in the face of the invasion by Iraq. We listened in silence. The broadcast dashed any hopes that, despite what we had witnessed that morning, there had been some mistake, that some maverick Iraqi army units had gone astray, that they would be called back and the situation returned to normal.

We went back inside the cafeteria to review the situation. There was real fear now. If the Iraqis were taking over Kuwait, when would they come for us? Would they launch artillery first? Would they respect our improvised white flags? Although I never mentioned it to anyone, I felt responsible for the tight spot that we were all in. If I had not insisted that the group come to the site the night before, if we had waited until the following morning, then we would not be caught out here in the desert like sitting ducks.

I imagined that the others were also thinking, "What if..." Osman was supposed to have been in Turkey to take care of some administrative matters, but he had delayed his trip to be on hand for the opening ceremony. Some of the engineers would normally have been in our Kuwait City offices, but had come out to the site specially for the event. But if that is what they were thinking, like me, they kept it to themselves. Instead, we tried to make light of the situation.

For instance, the ever enthusiastic Ozer Ozkan said that finally he would be able to cut an opening in the fence that ran between the living area and the administrative offices. That would cut the driving time between the two places by more than half. For some reason, the Kuwaiti ministry had rejected Ozer's repeated requests to carry out this idea. But, as he pointed out, it was highly unlikely that the Kuwaiti ministry could stop him now. For that, he said, we owed Saddam Hussein, so maybe we should send him a thank-you note.

The laughter continued when I pointed out that had it not been for the invasion, we at that moment would have been enduring all the stress of meeting with the Undersecretary and his entourage, making sure they were comfortable and happy. Now it was more than halfway through the day and business pressure was the furthest thing from our minds.

One of the construction workers pointed out a window. A line of tanks and armored vehicles, flying solid black banners and flags, was driving past the entrance to the site. When we got outside we saw that they were actually circling around the entire perimeter. I thought of the way the Shoshone or the Sioux would gallop around the covered wagons of the pioneers in American Wild West movies.

A jeep peeled off from a column of tanks and headed for the entrance to the site. It stopped a few hundred meters away and a number of soldiers stepped out and walked toward us. All were carrying automatic rifles with the distinctive banana clips of Kalashnikov AK-47s.

We walked through the gate and out into the open, waving our hands in greeting to show that we were not armed, our insides churning in anticipation of the worst. A few moments later, they were before us, high ranking officers, colonels evidently, and their aides. We were able to communicate using a mixture of Arabic, Turkish and English. Some of them appeared to be of Turkish origin.

I told them we were a Turkish firm, that we had nothing to do with the conflict, and that we hoped to be able to travel as soon as possible to the Turkish embassy in Kuwait City. The officers did not respond to that but were polite and respectful, asking us how many of us there were and what the nature of the project was. To keep on friendly terms, I invited them to come inside.

As we walked through the gate, Sedat suggested it might not be wise to take them inside the facilities and let them see all the amenities, that it might give them the idea of taking the place over for themselves. I agreed, so we arranged a table and chairs in the shade of the water tanks and served cold water and tea, which is all they asked for.

The meeting lasted only a short while. The officers continued to be low-key and polite as we explained a bit more about the work of our company. They gave no indication that they meant us any harm and when they left we felt more relaxed.

We wondered about the TJV staff back in Kuwait City and what was going on with them. Where were they? Had they been able to reach the office? Were they stuck at home, or stranded somewhere in the city?

After the Iraqi officers departed, a few of the regular Iraqi soldiers hesitantly stepped through the entrance to the site. They glanced around and saw us still seated at the table, but kept looking over their shoulders, evidently afraid of being spotted by their commanders. But thirst overcame their fear and they came to us begging for water. They were in a bad state, their uniforms torn and streaked with white stains from the salt released in their sweat, some of them exhibiting the symptoms of severe dehydration. They said they had been on the march all day without anything to drink.

As we filled their canteens and bottles with water and handed them back, we saw dozens more coming into the site, some of them in worse shape than the first ones, barely able to stay on their feet. Most still carried their weapons, but some seemed to have discarded their packs.

It is difficult to explain what thirst feels like in the desert. It is absolutely primal in its debilitating power, sucking away at the body's core and taking over the mind. No matter what one is doing, one part of the brain is constantly aware of the presence or absence of water. We thought there was no way that any of us could have marched for a day in such extreme heat without water.

Osman said to the others in our group, tongue in cheek, that we were always complaining about not having this thing or that thing on the job. But here was Iraq, able to transport an entire army into Kuwait, but unable to keep its troops properly supplied with water. Some of our group promised Osman they would never complain again. Somebody said, "Osman, you are definitely a better project manager than Saddam Hussein." Meanwhile, I wondered, if Iraq treated its soldiers so badly, what would happen if the Iraqi army were to confront real resistance?

We continued to distribute water to the soldiers lining up at the table and noticed that more were arriving, hundreds of them. We had started with a good amount of water in the tanks, but we became concerned as more and more soldiers arrived. One could survive for a while in these conditions without food, but not without water.

We therefore organized the distribution so that each soldier received a set amount of water, giving the explanation that we did not want to leave anyone out. Twice the officers returned to get more for themselves and we noted the way the soldiers would scramble to get out of their way, some even running behind the buildings. From the expressions on their faces, we could tell it was not out of respect, but out of fear. After the officers left, the soldiers would hurry back into line.

Some of the soldiers were too desperate to wait. One of our workers said soldiers were entering the site through a back entrance. I went around by the portable cabins to see what they were doing. These cabins rested on steel supports, about half a meter off the ground. I saw a pair of military boots sticking out from beneath one of them. When I bent over, I could see that the soldier was on his back, trying to suck moisture from the septic line running down through the floor of the cabin.

I grabbed his legs and tried to pull him away, but he would not let go of the pipe. Finally, I took a cup of water and splashed some on his legs. He quickly emerged and drank the rest in one swallow. Meanwhile, about a dozen more soldiers had crawled underneath cabins, and we had to promise them water before they would come out.

One of them turned out to be of Turkish origin. I asked him why the army did not provide its troops with sufficient water. He said that they always lacked water - that was just the way it was. He said that sometimes they would have to go without provisions for days at a time, that eventually you got used to it. Given what Iraqi soldiers had gone through during the desert war with Iran, I thought, the invasion of Kuwait must have seemed relatively easy.

Meanwhile, one of us would go inside the cafeteria every hour or so to listen for the news on the radio. We were careful to be discreet so that the Iraqis would not discover it. The officers had not ordered a search of the site, but we knew they might at any time and we could not afford to be without the radio. It was our only link to the world. We joked that the Middle East version of the American Express slogan should be "Don't leave home without a radio." Someone even suggested that American Express should produce dual-function credit cards, capable of receiving radio transmissions.

To make sure that we would not run out of batteries for the radio, we went around the site gathering all the appropriately sized ones we could find. Fortunately, we were able to put together a substantial supply.

The reports from international sources about Kuwait City were chilling and only increased our concern for our TJV colleagues there. We heard that Iraqi forces had seized Kuwaiti government buildings and banks, and that a number of top government figures had been arrested. One report said that a member of Kuwait's ruling Al-Sabah family had been hanged.

Starved of information, we tried to tune into as many radio stations as we could. We found two that were broadcasting in English from Kuwait. One of them was clearly controlled by Iraq: it enthusiastically announced the formation of a new government and referred to itself as the station of "Free Kuwait." The other one was still under the control of allies of the Al-Sabah family. Its announcers proclaimed that Kuwait could never be taken over by Iraq and called on all Kuwaitis to resist. Given what we had heard from other sources and what we had experienced that day ourselves, it was difficult to take this seriously. We wondered if they were really broadcasting from inside Kuwait.

The sun went down and darkness crept across the desert floor, but Iraqi soldiers kept coming for water. By now we had settled into a routine for dealing with them and we were able to distribute the water in an orderly manner. At the same time, the explosions we had heard throughout most of the day had tapered off and we were beginning to enjoy at least a semblance of normality.

Some of the engineers joked about the delays we had encountered in constructing the main water line into the site. Ozer, Ibrahim and Taner Papila had been directly involved, enduring all the bureaucratic delays and seemingly arbitrary changes made by the Ministry along the way. Taner, in his thirties and the youngest among the engineers, was the worrying type, always imagining the worst. He'd been saying for months that the Kuwaitis would never let us get the water lines running.

As of that day, the system was finally ready to be made operational and it was supposed to have been part of the ceremony. And we were going to have to open the main valve the next morning anyway, because the Iraqi soldiers were depleting the supply in the tanks. The irony was that after all the Ministry's supervision and concern, the new water system would end up benefiting the Iraqi army.

Our laughter subsided, however, as we tracked the broadcasts of the BBC, the Voice of America, the Voice of Turkey and even the Diyarbakir station in Turkey that we were able to tune it at times. It was now being reported that U.S. aircraft carrier groups were steaming from the Indian Ocean toward the Gulf and that U.S. military air units in the region were being beefed up as well. The construction site was on the north shore of the Gulf just across the bridge from Bubiyan Island, home to an important Kuwaiti military base. If the Americans counterattacked to drive the Iraqis out of Kuwait we would be in the middle of everything. The thought was chilling.

The Iraqi officers returned and were quite boastful in telling us that Iraqi forces were bringing Kuwait City "to its knees," running over anything and anyone who got in their way. This heightened our concern for all our friends: Turks, Kuwaitis, Britons, Americans and others in the international community there.

On the early evening news broadcasts we heard that Kuwait City was mostly under the control of the Iraqis and that Saddam Hussein was threatening to "turn Kuwait into a graveyard" if there were any international intervention.

Until that point we were still pondering the possibility of somehow slipping through the Iraqi military cordon around the site and trying to escape to Kuwait City. But now, we realized that other alternatives would have to be considered. Some in our group wondered if it might be worth trying to negotiate with the Iraqi officers, to see if they would provide an escort for us from the site to the Turkish embassy in the city.

Taner, his eyeglasses as always giving him a studious look, spread out a detailed map of the Middle East. He suggested that it might be possible to head north across the border into the city of Basra in southern Iraq, then to Baghdad, then on to Habur at the Turkish border. The route was long, complicated and dangerous and some wondered if Taner was serious. But Taner was rarely anything but serious.

To lighten things up, I said that Taner's proposed route might be worth it if only to see Baghdad. I told everyone how beautiful I had found the city when I had been there a number of years ago. Mehmet Cetinkoprulu, who for three years had been the manager of a construction site in Baghdad for the Kutlutas Company, agreed that Baghdad was splendid, especially the food. We were soon daydreaming about eating the delicious variety of whitefish found in the currents of the Dicle River. In Iraq, of course, the river is called the Tigris. But

23

we called it the Dicle, its name in Turkey, where its waters originate.

We decided it was best not to act precipitously, and to remain at the site at least for a while to see if things would settle down or if other opportunities would arise. It was now after midnight and the hordes of Iraqi soldiers had finally stopped coming for water. We shut down the electrical generators for the night, fearing that any lights might attract attention or make the site a possible target for a military attack.

With the power off, and therefore the air-conditioning, we slept outside, the engineers on mattresses all in a row. The construction workers were scattered here and there, some putting their mattresses on the roof of the cafeteria, others on the sloping ground beneath the water tanks.

A full moon rose up from the desert while swaths of stars painted the galactic dome. As we lay on our backs, taking in this spectacle, Ozer identified constellations - the Great Bear, Orion the Hunter - and pointed out the North Star at the end of the handle of the Little Dipper, explaining how it could be used for navigation. It helped us to relax, to wind down from a shattering day.

Taner, however, was still anxious, saying over and over that his parents would have heart attacks if they knew of our predicament. We told him that everyone's families naturally would be worried but it was probably best not to dwell on it and to stay calm.

I told the group that it was in fact the first time in months that I had felt so relaxed. When they looked at me strangely, I said, "Really, think about it - no more deadlines, no more difficult meetings with bankers, no more pressures, what more could I want?" They started laughing, so I kept on, saying that it was terrific being free of all that responsibility, and in just one day too. By the time I was saying I wanted to send something nice to Saddam Hussein for bringing me this great relief, I think even Taner was laughing. At the same time, though, I was thinking to myself that I would gladly endure any kind of business pressure in exchange for a way out of this jam.

Osman said it was time for some ice cream. I thought he was continuing with the jokes. I did not know that a batch of vanilla ice cream had been brought in specially for the inaugural ceremony. So, before we nodded off to sleep, it was ice cream for everyone under the stars, punctuated by the occasional explosion in the distance.

Friday, August 3rd, 1990

It was the start of the weekend in Kuwait. We were all awake early, showering, shaving, and sitting down to breakfast by 6:30 am. After eating, we filled thermos bottles with hot water and prepared packages of coffee, tea and sugar for the day, trying to make it business as usual, while knowing all along that nothing could have been further from the truth.

The radio brought more ominous news. We heard reports that Iraq had closed the borders of both Iraq and Kuwait and that foreigners were not being allowed to leave either country. Martial law had been declared in Kuwait; no one was allowed to be outside after sundown; and the Kuwaiti telephone system was being shut down.

We wondered how our TJV people were faring in Kuwait City and figured they were probably wondering what had become of us. Had Musteba or Asim, our mechanical engineers in charge of coordination between the construction site and the main office, contacted the Turkish embassy to inform them we had been stranded? Did our embassy have any information? Had the Undersecretary or his deputy, Mr. Al-Enizi, contacted our embassy about us, or had they been arrested by Iraqi forces? Many questions, no answers.

And we wondered if there was any way we could get word to our families that we were in a difficult situation, but still okay.

It was not long before Iraqi soldiers started coming back for water, and by the hundreds - more of them than the day before, it seemed. They appeared mentally and physically beat. We'd fill their containers, they'd swallow the water down in one gulp, it seemed, then we'd fill them again. Their minds were focused on one thing - water.

Then the officers returned, so we brought out the chairs again and served them tea and coffee. With their commanders present, the soldiers again stayed away.

A short time later, Ozer burst into the cafeteria grinning broadly. He said he had convinced one of the Iraqi officers to let him drive to the other side of the site to open the main water valve. He was even being allowed to cut the fence and shorten the distance, as he'd been wanting to do for weeks. He ran out with a pair of wire cutters. He was even more excited when he returned, because the officer had told him that the Iraqi units would soon escort us back to the TJV office in Kuwait City.

Invigorated by this news, we started planning our departure. Taner, however, still thought the best idea was to get out of Kuwait. If the Iraqis were willing to escort us someplace, he asked, why couldn't they take us into Iraq? Then we could travel to Turkey by the route he had mapped out the day before. After some discussion, we shelved that idea because it sounded too risky and because we did not want to desert our colleagues in Kuwait City. Moreover, if we could reach Kuwait City, the Turkish embassy would have wireless communication to send word to our families. Presumably, it was still protected by diplomatic immunity.

At that point a small convoy of military vehicles arrived, led by another of the Iraqi officers we had met the day before. He told us to prepare to leave immediately, that the area was no longer safe, that we were being taken to a secure place. We insisted that we be taken to the Turkish embassy, but he said that he would have to take us to the base of his commanding officer first. Once we had been registered there, he said, we would be able to go wherever we wanted.

The officer signaled for a canvas-topped truck, apparently a troop carrier, and urged us to board immediately. I turned, stepped quickly into my sleeping cabin and started packing a change of clothes into my briefcase. An Iraqi soldier came in right behind me, finger on the trigger of his AK-47. By the time I was shutting my case, there were four of them. They proceeded to search the room.

When I came out, nearly everyone else was in the truck. I refused to get in. I told the officer that our group would leave the site in our own vehicles or not leave at all. He pondered this for a tense moment, then agreed. The engineers then boarded our Pajero jeep, while our construction workers got in the minibus. The two Egyptian security guards were put in the military truck.

The military truck left the site at the head of the caravan, followed by the jeep, the minibus, and then more military vehicles. As we departed, we saw swarms of soldiers starting to go through the buildings on the site. Whatever optimism we had felt was evaporating. As some of us turned to take a last look at the site through the billowing clouds of dust in our wake, Mehmet Cetinkoprulu said, "A new version of Midnight Express (the gut-wrenching Alan Parker film about imprisonment) is beginning."

As we approached the intersection of the main north-south road, where we had been turned back the day before, the question was, which way would we go? Left to Kuwait City, or right toward Iraq? Our future seemed to have boiled down to a simple turn on a highway.

The lead truck turned right. We were not going to Kuwait City.

I heard someone in the back of the jeep say, "Basra." But then we turned off the pavement and onto a road that was being carved into the desert by heavy construction equipment operated by Iraqi soldiers. The jeep was jolted up and down as we struggled to keep up with the truck on the rugged terrain. Ozer was driving, peering through swirls of dust kicked up by the truck. I sat next to him, while the other engineers were cramped in the back. The few belongings we had been able to pack before leaving were in the trunk, including our cold water barrel. No-one spoke.

We passed dozens of bulldozers, loaders and other equipment excavating on both sides of the road, preparing foundations for structures of some sort. Camouflage rigging was being erected to cover military vehicles. It seemed the Iraqi military was digging in for the long haul.

The truck pulled up in front of a tent and the officers who had taken us from the construction site consulted with what appeared to be their superiors. One asked if we had any water. We said yes, not really having much choice in the matter, and brought out our barrel. By the time the first officer had finished drinking, there were another two dozen lined up behind him. If we made it out of this alive, I thought, I would send the Iraqi government a bill for providing water to its troops.

The officers decided we were at the wrong place, so we drove off again, now led by one of the new officers in a jeep. Continuing through the desert, we observed thousands of soldiers, some on the move, some making camp. Anti-aircraft batteries and howitzers were being put in place.

We stopped at a number of other tents. There were more consultations between officers and it seemed they didn't know what to do with us. Then we came to what appeared to be some type of headquarters, with a number of tents, a lot of vehicles and a water tank.

We stepped out of the Pajero and the minibus to be lined up and counted. We pronounced our names and the officers would try to write them down in Arabic. Then we were told to get back into the vehicles and the little caravan headed off again. We continued to pass large deployments of troops, weaponry and construction equipment. We joked that if we were ever set free, we could provide quite a bit of intelligence. I thought to myself, however, that if they were planning to release us they would not have allowed us to witness this breathtaking military mobilization.

The lead jeep stopped in the middle of nowhere and a number of soldiers got out of the truck and ordered us to sit on the ground. I refused. It was probably crazy to do something so risky, but I was getting annoyed with the way we were being jerked around.   Some of the other engineers remained standing. The soldiers started yelling and gesturing at us to get down. Later, we agreed that we needed to keep better control of ourselves - any one of these Iraqis could have an itchy trigger finger.

An officer walked over and said something in rapid Arabic that made the soldiers calm down. They then proceeded to conduct another head count, with some of us sitting and some standing, as we said our names and watched the soldiers trying to write them down. Amazingly, the soldiers then took out some matches and set fire to the list of names they had just recorded. As we watched it burn on the sand, we wondered what was going on? If they were aiming to heighten our fear, they were succeeding.

Ozer pointed out that the tires on the Pajero were becoming dangerously worn. Originally, I had wanted all of the Turkish engineers and workers in one vehicle anyway, so we decided to abandon the jeep and have all of us on the bus.

While I was waiting for the others to climb in, I noticed that the overweight Egyptian security guard, who had been riding in the truck, was talking to one of the officers in a very deferential manner, apparently begging him for something. Someone joked that if they allowed the Egyptian into the minibus, they would have to leave half of us behind. All of a sudden, the Egyptian grabbed the officer's hand and appeared to be thanking him profusely. It seemed they were going to release him.

There was also a thin man with a huge suitcase, who had been riding in the truck as well, apparently picked up somewhere along the way. One of the officers motioned for him to get on the bus with us. He turned out to be a Bangladeshi. With him, plus an armed soldier, there were nearly forty people stuffed into this twenty-passenger vehicle.

Our driver, Mehmet, was behind the wheel. I sat in the other front seat and Ozer sat on the water barrel in between us. Ahmet Nakiboglu, another of our engineers and the production manager on the Sabiya project, squeezed in between the barrel and me. In his thirties and with a thin mustache, Ahmet was easy-going yet very proper, preferring to keep his suspenders and jacket on no matter how high the temperature climbed.

The other engineers wedged themselves into the rows behind us, with the Bangladeshi man and the construction workers in the back, some having to stand with their shoulders bowed in the narrow aisle. One of the officers got into the Pajero and the soldier on the bus told Mehmet to follow him. As we neared the main road, we stopped for two more soldiers to jam themselves in. The Pajero went off in another direction and disappeared from sight.

At the main road the soldiers weren't sure which way to go. They argued for a while in Arabic, then pointed left. We made the turn, toward the south, and there were renewed hopes that we were going to Kuwait City. But they had Mehmet pull over so they could consult with the drivers of some armored vehicles. Then they ordered him to make a wide U-turn until, once again, we were heading north toward Iraq.

The air-conditioning continued to function, but was not strong enough to cool the air with so many people crammed inside. It was now 10:30 am and the temperature was again climbing toward 50 degrees Centigrade. A road sign told us that it was three hundred kilometers to Basra. Seemingly endless military convoys passed us going south, deeper into Kuwait. Some of the vehicles were transporting troops and artillery; others carried tanks.

We began making comparisons between the Iraqi military and the Turkish military. It seemed that the Iraq military was far more mobile and capable of moving large numbers of troops and great quantities of equipment over long distances. At one point, as the road passed near the Gulf, we saw what appeared to be Iraqi ships transporting even more tanks and other military hardware. At the same time, there was very little cover in the Kuwaiti desert. There were no towns or settlements; Iraqi units would be highly vulnerable to the type of carpet bombing the U.S. and its NATO allies were capable of carrying out.

One of the soldiers on the bus changed places with Ahmet and sat on the water barrel. I asked him his name and he told me it was Ali. I said that I was named Ali too. He was very thin, not more than twenty years old, and generally polite. He spoke a little English. I thought that it probably hadn't been long since

32

he'd left home. But his sun-darkened skin and the practiced way he handled his AK-47 told me he had been in the army for some time.

By late morning we had crossed into Iraq at Umm Qasr, a small city just on the other side of the border from Kuwait and Iraq's only Persian Gulf port. The harbor area, fed by a railway, was a hive of activity, a major hub of Iraq's military effort.

We reached Basra a few hours later. Again the soldiers did not know which way to go, telling Mehmet to take one road, then another, until we were lost in the streets of the city, trying to find our way back to the main road. The soldiers would tell Mehmet to stop, approach perplexed pedestrians for directions, then bicker some more among themselves. They tried asking some of their compatriots manning guard posts along the way, but they could not help either. Meanwhile, we were running low on water and what was left in the barrel was warm. In Basra's afternoon heat, we were starting to become very thirsty.

A group of soldiers at a major intersection pointed us toward a guard house down the road. It marked the entrance to a military installation of some sort. Once inside, we drove toward a grandstand, part of a small stadium where there were many buses and cars, most of which had Kuwaiti plates.

We pulled up in the front of the grandstand and one of the soldiers went inside. We thought this might be a place where Kuwaiti prisoners of war taken during the invasion were being held. If so, we hoped that once we were found to be Turks, we would be released. But that dream quickly dissolved when the soldier returned. He motioned for Mehmet to get in the back, slid in behind the wheel, and drove the bus back out onto the streets. I asked the soldier named Ali why we were leaving. He said because this was the wrong place.

33

The soldier now driving the bus kept pulling on his thin, curling mustache as he turned this way and that looking for something but obviously not finding it. The mustache made me think he might be of Turkish descent. Occasionally we would come to a familiar intersection and members of our group would yell out, "Hey, we've already been here!"

Our shouting seemed to rattle the soldiers, and the one who was driving, who seemed to lack experience of operating a minibus, nearly collided with other vehicles a number of times in the teeming Basra traffic. He stopped along one street, and all the soldiers got out. All except one went off, apparently to get directions. Inside the bus, we considered trying to escape, but decided there was still a possibility we would be released and it was not worth the risk.

When the soldiers got back on the bus, we insisted that Mehmet be allowed to drive, for the safety of everyone. Finally, they gave in, when we said, "Look, we're not going to escape because you are the ones with the guns."

The water was now depleted and our thirst was mounting. Also, the minibus was nearly out of gasoline. When we pulled into a filling station, some of us headed toward the grocery store next door. The soldiers yelled for us to stop but we entered the store anyway. We did not have Iraqi dinars and the owner said they did not accept Kuwaiti dinars. He said U.S. dollars would be fine. We had enough to buy a few cases of cold Coca Cola.

The soldiers now seemed to think they knew where they were going. They managed to get us back onto the main road and every now and then they would direct Mehmet to turn down a side street. We would eventually come to some imposing structure with iron doors and wire fences. Invariably, we would be turned away.

We arrived at one military camp on the desolate outskirts of the city. As at every other camp, there was a portrait of Saddam Hussein painted on a stone wall to greet us. But what really caught our eye were two large tents with open sides packed with any amount of televisions, refrigerators, sound systems and bicycles. We wondered if it was war plunder, brought in from Kuwait to be distributed to the Iraqi military.

At another camp, there were two soldiers standing guard who turned out to be of Turkish descent. One of them was named Abbas, my father's name. Both of them spoke some Turkish. They tried to reassure us that once we found the right military base to be registered, we would be released because we had nothing to do with this conflict and relations between Turkey and Iraq were okay.

There seemed to be no end to the confusion over what to do about us. We wondered whether the entire Iraqi military could be this disorganized. We began to refer to ourselves as the "Unwanted Prisoners," and started to laugh out loud every time the soldiers argued about what to do next.

Ahmet Nakiboglu said that it was truly amazing that with all the prisons in Iraq they couldn't find one to accept us. Exasperated, he said to one of the soldiers, "Look, we're all very tired, why don't you just take us to any place at all tonight and worry about finding the correct location tomorrow?"

Mehmet Cetinkoprulu said that if we were Americans every military base and prison would be jumping at the chance to take us.

At two of the military installations, we overheard the soldiers referring to us as hostages. The word for hostages is practically the same in Turkish as in Arabic. After hearing them use this term, we confronted them, asking why they were calling us that. They denied it, saying that the term they were

35

using referred to the specific military base they were trying to find. That did not ease our minds at all.

The Bangladeshi man was becoming a nuisance. Every time we stopped, he dragged his huge suitcase out of the bus, then dragged it back on when we left. It should not have been a big deal, but it seemed like more time wasting when we were all increasingly frustrated and on edge.

Anti-aircraft missile batteries were deployed at one base where we stopped and, having heard the soldiers use the word hostages, we imagined being held there as shields against aerial attack. We got out of the bus, fear now competing with exhaustion. We had been awake since very early in the morning and our muscles were cramping from being packed into the bus all day.

We were approached by some soldiers who spoke a bit of Turkish. They brought us some water. It was brackish, apparently because this far south in Iraq the salt water of the Gulf mingled with the waters of the Tigris. Some of us complained, but Ahmet said that in this incredible heat, with everyone sweating so profusely, it was a good thing to be replenishing the salt in our systems.

All of a sudden, Taner became very excited. One of the Turkish-speaking soldiers had offered to make a phone call for us. Taner said we should write down all our numbers, give them to this soldier and maybe give him some money too. Some of the group wondered why the guy would be willing to do that for us and warned that he might just pocket the money and call no-one.

As we were ordered back onto the minibus, the soldier approached one of the windows. He asked if we had the numbers for him to call. The bus, driven again by one of the soldiers, was starting to leave. Taner hurriedly wrote down his phone number and gave it to the soldier as we started to pull away. Maybe now our families would be able to hear that we were alive, at least.

But as the bus exited the base, Taner yelled out, "Oh, no!" He said that the number he had given the soldier was connected to an answering machine and that if the caller didn't wait for the third beep, the message would not be recorded.

At first we were deeply disappointed. But after a while the absurdity of the whole thing overwhelmed us and we laughed out loud. Was some Iraqi soldier really going to risk his life to make a telephone call from an Iraqi military base to tell someone that Taner and his friends were being driven around Basra by the Iraqi army?

We noticed that the bus was moving away from center of the city again. Mehmet Cetinkoprulu said we were heading east, toward the nearby border with Iran. He wondered whether our destination was one of the dreaded detention centers where Iranian prisoners had been jailed during the war between Iraq and Iran in the 1980s.

Hearing this from Mehmet, I began to wonder whether we were coming to the final stop, from which we would not get out alive. Ozer, apparently thinking the same thing, said that this might be our last chance to try to overpower the soldiers and drive the minibus back to our embassy in Kuwait. Some of the others said it might be possible to disarm the soldiers, but did we really want to drive back through those massive Iraqi military deployments in the Kuwaiti desert?

As we moved further away from Basra, tanks and other military vehicles began appearing along the side the road. Finally, at about 11 pm, we entered a military compound with a number of sectors separated by barbed wire. All kinds of military vehicles moved along the roads inside this base. We parked amidst a number of civilian buses with Kuwaiti plates and brown Iraqi military buses, all filled with civilians.

We got off the minibus to stretch our legs, when suddenly we heard voices shouting and boots pounding on the gravelly earth. A group of Iraqi soldiers, firearms at the ready, were chasing a man in civilian clothes, who was running toward the darkness at the edge of the compound. When he ignored their order to stop, they opened fire and he fell heavily to the ground, screaming and writhing in pain.

Mehmet Cetinkoprulu said, "You see, the movie has started."

We all scrambled back onto the bus and ducked for cover. Ahmet, who had said he was willing to stay at any camp at all, said he would never complain again as long as we didn't have to stay in this one. Peaking through the windows of the bus, we saw Iraqi soldiers hauling the wounded man away, his cries still audible even after he disappeared from sight. A few minutes later, Ali and the other soldiers said we were leaving, to our great relief.

It was almost midnight and we had been hauled around Basra for nearly ten hours, our emotions swinging back and forth between frustration, hysteria and fear. Now we were back out on the desert road, the minibus banging from side to side through jagged holes and ruts.

We finally found ourselves back at the remote camp where we had seen the tents full of televisions, appliances and other goods. The soldiers spent some time consulting with the officers there, then told us we would be spending the night. But there was nothing there - no buildings, no beds, nothing. We thought they were crazy and complained loudly that we had not eaten since morning and were out of water. I rebuked the soldiers, saying that their treatment of us was intolerable.

A short while later, Ali showed up with two blankets that he spread out on the sand. Some in our group were so tired they lay down immediately.

I stayed in the minibus. When one of the soldiers told me to get out, I asked why. He said he had to take the vehicle somewhere to have it searched. I told him that if he moved the bus I was staying in it because all our belongings were inside. And if he wanted to search it he could do it right there.

To my disbelief they backed off, moved the bus only a few meters away, and then got out. I thought maybe the "search" they wanted to carry out was not about security, but about trying to exploit the opportunity to steal our belongings.

With this in mind, I decided to sleep in the bus. Before I nodded off, I noticed a soldier sitting by the tents with a machine gun. Some time later, I was jolted awake by the sound of snoring so loud that I thought anti-aircraft batteries were being fired. Instead, it was Taner, who had climbed into the bus after I had fallen asleep. I tried waking him, but to no avail.

A soldier asked me how many of us were sleeping in the bus and I told him two. A while later, another soldier, very agitated and swinging his rifle around, woke me to ask where the other man was. Taner was indeed not there and for a moment I wondered if he had tried to escape. But when I called his name, it turned out he had moved outside, onto one of the blankets.

Exhausted as we were, hunger kept waking us. Finally, I yelled out to the soldier Ali, berating him in a combination of Arabic and English for dragging us all over Basra without giving us any food. He looked apologetic, held out his hands palms up and shrugged.

I fell back to sleep but was awakened a short time later by Ali saying that he had brought me some bread. I told him that all of us needed food, not just me. He went away and returned with more bread, as well as some watermelon and canned cheese. It was not much but it was enough for each of us to have a little.

Saturday, August 4th, 1990

I woke up inside the minibus at about 5:30 am. Those who had slept outside on the blankets were stretching and rubbing their backs and shoulders. It was the first time any of them had ever slept on sand. They had used what few belongings they had as pillows. The sun had not yet risen, but the sand was still warm from the previous day. We could feel that it was going to be another hot day. So early in the morning, it felt like it was already pushing 35 degrees Centigrade.

The soldiers brought us more bread and canned cheese. Ali was trying to open the can of cheese with his side arm. He seemed to be trying to make up for putting us through this ordeal. Using his limited English and touching his shoulders in a crude form of sign language, he told us that an officer or commander of some sort was expected.

So we waited. The sun began to rise and it got progressively hotter. We could not all fit in the rapidly shrinking shade of the minibus. There was a single tree not too far away, but we had used it as a latrine during the night because the tiny, sheet-iron outhouse had no septic tank and was overflowing. There was a water jug with a handle and a long spout, but it was empty.

Two of the Iraqi soldiers came over, the one called Abbas we had met the day before, and another named Omer, who also spoke some Turkish. They said they had been drafted into the army, that all Iraqi males must serve three years. A third soldier, who also spoke some Turkish, came over and I spoke with him. I asked him about his salary and was stunned when he said it was only $10 a month. Moreover, he had not received any pay whatsoever for ten years. In effect, he was serving in the army for room and board. The other soldiers got angry with him for telling me this and ordered me to go sit on the other side of the tree. A few minutes later, the third soldier had disappeared. We never saw him again.

I considered what had happened the day before in Basra. I remembered vividly the murals of Saddam Hussein. In every square and at every military camp, there had been a two-meter by three-meter wall erected with Saddam's likeness painted on it. He seemed to be wearing a different outfit in every portrait. Sometimes he appeared as a soldier and other times as a civilian. In the military bases the murals would feature Saddam firing a machine gun or standing on a tank.

It became a great source of amusement for us. We decided that Saddam was like a one-model fashion show. Besides, the portraits were done in an amateurish way. You could tell it was supposed to be Saddam, but in some of the murals he appeared to have been rendered by a house painter, not an artist.

I also thought about the stories of the heat in Basra that had been handed down by our Turkish ancestors since the time when Basra was part of the Ottoman Empire. It almost defies description; you cannot really understand the intensity until you have experienced it yourself. The hot wind was like a giant, electric hairdryer blowing in our faces. Bare skin would begin to burn after only a few minutes of exposure. So, like whirling dervishes, we kept spinning around. Somebody said we had become chickens cooking on a spit. A few in the group sought relief beneath the tree, despite the use we had put it to the night before.

Osman suggested we constructed a tent, using the tripods from the surveying equipment we still had in the minibus, a few stray metal rods and the blankets. We could not find a heavy stone to use as an anchor, so we used the Bangladeshi man's suitcase - finally it had become useful after all.

We tried to get comfortable under the tent, some of us wetting towels and putting them on our heads, others trying to dampen their clothes. Leaning back, I looked up and saw that Ahmet Nakiboglu had climbed the tree and was perched on a branch, looking like an African lion.

Mehmet Cetinkoprulu brought out a white scarf with a red polka dot pattern, the type that Palestinians wear, and wrapped it around his head. Mehmet, who looked like a Palestinian anyway, was always being asked about his nationality. But this was neither the time nor the place to be mistaken for a Palestinian, so we asked him not to wear the scarf, at least for the time being.

We continued to wait, but no officer or commander arrived. We were getting increasingly anxious, losing patience, but at the same time realizing that maybe no-one would be coming to release us amid all the confusion - that we had better start getting used to the situation.

The wet scarves and towels around our people's heads were drying up in a matter of minutes and we were constantly thirsty. If somebody had poured water continuously into our mouth, it would still not have been enough to satisfy us. On top of that, the water we had was salty. We had managed to obtain some ice from the soldiers' tent, but the salty water was making us even more thirsty. It was unlike anything we had ever experienced, a feeling of literally drying up.

The Iraqi soldier called Omer came over to where we were sitting. We asked for fresh water, ice, and watermelon and even offered him money. But he would not take it, saying that no more water would be available until the next morning.

An officer appeared and we thought we might finally get moving from this place. But he just exchanged a few words with the solders guarding us. We offered him money to have some water and food brought to us but he wouldn't take it either. So we appeared to be stuck, going nowhere, with no food and a only a bit of salty water to counter the dehydrating effects of the heat.

When we complained to the soldier called Ali, he said that the conditions were the same for him and there was nothing he could do. He said at one point that he had been living like this for months. We responded that he was a soldier, while we were civilians, that we had no choice, that we had been brought here by force. I did not know how much he understood of what we were saying, but he seemed embarrassed, maybe even a little ashamed, when the construction workers tried to convey our meaning.

As we continued to wait, on the edge of despair, the officer arrived who had originally sent us to Basra, Ali's commanding officer. This gave us a lift because he already knew who we were and spoke enough English to communicate with us directly. He told us that he would contact the right people, clear up the confusion and have us moved to where we were supposed to be within half an hour. Just as we were telling him about the lack of food and water, one of the soldiers showed up with some water, watermelon, and a few other things to eat.

The sun was rising further and we started shifting the angle of the tent to protect ourselves from its powerful rays. Our driver Mehmet, who comes from the Black Sea region of Turkey, requested that he be allowed to "slip away," meaning try to escape. We thought it might not be a bad idea, although it might have been even better if he had gone on a reconnaissance mission the night before, to get an idea of how the camp was laid out and how someone might get past the guards.

While we had been driving around in Basra, we had seen Turkish trucks and Mehmet said he could find them again. He said he was ready to go now. We said we would let him know when the time was right and told him not to leave until then. We told him not to leave without getting definite approval from us.

Meanwhile, we continued to wait. Every now and then Mehmet would come to us with a plan - how he would sneak away in this direction or that. The way we saw it, he would have to walk or crawl about 600 meters without being seen and then get to cover on the other side of a large sand dune.

Mehmet started taking short walks away from our tent, apparently testing the vigilance of the guards. It didn't work; it only aroused suspicion. Ali and other soldiers came over and warned him to sit down and stay down. A short while later, we heard Ali start yelling, "Where is Mehmet?" We looked around, didn't see him and thought he'd gone off and would be caught.

It turned out, however, that he was only on the other side of the tree. We breathed a sigh of relief. Who knows what kind of trouble we would have been in if he actually had tried to escape? And what would they have done to him if he had failed?

Just then, a jeep appeared in the distance. Trapped in the middle of the desert with hardly any water and feeling increasingly desperate, the sight of a vehicle approaching made us all excited. Indeed, we were told we would be moving immediately and to get into the minibus.

Accompanied by the jeep, we traveled back in the direction we had come the day before, eventually arriving at one of the very same camps we had been turned away from. In unison we cried, "No, no, no, we've come to the wrong place again!"

It looked like a typical prison camp, an empty square in the middle surrounded by an expanse of single-story buildings in a U-shaped pattern. The soldiers in the jeep consulted the camp commanders, then ordered us to get out with all our belongings. The minibus was driven away and that was the last we would see of it.

We were taken down roads that cut through the camp and eventually came to a group of poorly constructed, single-story buildings. Hundreds of people were being held in front of them, including Kuwaiti soldiers, which we did not find encouraging.

We were pressed into line and taken single file toward a table manned by soldiers in the shadow of one of the buildings. The soldiers called out our names one by one and tried to write them down phonetically in Arabic. They then searched our belongings, but not very carefully. They didn't look in my bag at all and so they missed the little tape recorder I was using to record my journal.

At that point, the radio was the most valuable item we possessed. Neither the minibus, the money in our pockets, nor any money we may have had in a bank somewhere meant as much to us as that radio, which couldn't have cost more than ten dollars. The construction worker who had brought it along had done an excellent job of concealing it. So when the search was finished and the radio had not been discovered, we all smiled at each other, knowing we would still be able to listen in the evenings to the BBC, the Voice of America, Diyarbakir Radio and the Voice of Turkey.

The scenarios we tried to imagine for ourselves would go back and forth between optimistic and pessimistic, depending on what we had heard last on that radio. The most recent news was that the situation remained tense, there was continued diplomatic activity with world leaders consulting one another, and American warships were steaming toward the Gulf.

Eventually all of our group, engineers and construction workers, had been to the table and had their names registered by the soldiers. It seemed now to be official: we were hostages of the Iraqi regime. Next, we were taken to our prison quarters, one of the numerous cramped single-room structures in this place, about five-by-ten meters, with one small window in front, the floors half concrete and half rocky earth.

The heat inside was brutal, so most of the prisoners stayed outside. Inside our building there was a Kuwaiti trying desperately to cool himself with a damp and dirty piece of cloth, looking as if he was about to pass out. We also found two overweight Kuwaiti soldiers, wearing only shorts, who told us in English they had been there for a couple of days. When they noticed we had cold water, they begged for some. I asked them if they were given water by the guards. They said they were, but not often and it was warm.

I looked at my colleagues. In the course of doing business I frequently made decisions that millions of dollars rode upon, but in this case I wasn't sure how to respond. Some of our group objected, saying we had to preserve our supply. I told the Kuwaiti soldiers that if they were not brought water soon, we would give them some of ours. In the end, we did.

We asked them why the Kuwaiti army had surrendered to the Iraqis without putting up a fight. One of them said, "Swear to God, Kuwaiti soldiers didn't know anything about what was happening. We were captured and brought here; that's all we know." They said that their commanders were in another building and that they would know more about what had happened.

Members of our group began to move around and talk with other prisoners. Eventually we concluded that there were maybe two thousand held in this camp. There were people of many nationalities, including Indian, Pakistani, Chinese, Korean, Sri Lankan, Saudi Arabian, Philippino and Kuwaiti, including Kuwaiti soldiers.

Kuwaiti officers were indeed being housed in a separate building and it was said that they had bunks and air-conditioning. We thought it ridiculous that the Iraqis would provide their enemies with such comfort, while jamming sixty to seventy innocent civilians into a single, filthy room.

Our room was in fact so cramped that it could not fit all those assigned to it even if we all remained standing. That was probably why we were allowed to wander freely outside the buildings. In any case, the entire compound was surrounded by barbed wire and fully armed soldiers.

Now that there was no longer any question of our status as hostages, we began to try everything we could think of to get word to the Turkish embassy in Baghdad. We persuaded one of the Iraqi officers who had brought us here to inform the commander of this prison camp that I held important positions in Turkey. It was suggested to him that the Turkish government would be very interested in my report of how we were being treated in Iraq.

The officer asked me if I had a diplomatic passport. In fact, I did not but I kept silent for a moment while I thought how to respond. When he repeated the question, my fellow engineers answered at once, "Yes, he has a diplomatic passport!"

When the officer left, my colleagues reminded me that many of our group were without their passports, having left them in Kuwait City when we had traveled to Sabiya. To confirm that I had a diplomatic passport, the Iraqis would have to contact our embassy. That way our government would find out that we were being held. Less than an hour later, a soldier came to take me to the camp commander. We hoped that our gambit was going to pay off.

The commander's office was located near the front of the camp. As I entered, he was seated inside with a few other officers, one of whom was bilingual in English and Arabic and helped to translate our conversation as an old air-conditioner struggled to cool the air. The commander offered me some food and water and apologized for our treatment during what he called this time of war. He said that things would soon be back to normal and that he would be able to release us if not today then tomorrow.

I did not believe him. Thus far we had heard nothing but false promises and lies, all apparently designed to keep us quiet while we were held captive. Firmly and in no uncertain terms, I explained to him that they were making a mistake - that they needed to inform the Turkish embassy of our presence in this camp immediately. If they did not, then Iraq's ties with Turkey would suffer. The officer who was translating tried to calm me by suggesting that my views would be seriously considered and communicated to higher-ranking officers.

Back at our quarters, my colleagues and I noted that most of the others held in this camp were also civilians from different parts of the world, people who had been working for various companies and firms in Kuwait at the time of the invasion. They had nothing to do with this war and, like us, they were trying to figure out what the Iraqis were going to do with them. Many of the newly arrived prisoners had been seized from their offices and workplaces in Kuwait City and were miserable because their families had no idea where they were or why they were there.

Meanwhile, since arriving at this camp, our group had been given no food. Near a military vehicle which exuded a terribly foul odor, we saw stacks of large empty trays and big buckets. We anticipated the worst. The camp had only two spigots with running water and some of our construction workers joined the lines of hundreds of people waiting to fill assorted containers. Their patience and ability to adapt to these dire conditions were admirable.

That night we were introduced to the stale bread that we would be eating in the days to come. It was the size of sandwich bread, but incredibly hard, nearly impossible to break, let alone chew. After a while, we learned to ingest it by soaking it with water in our mouths.

Having traveled for hours over bumpy roads I was feeling increasing pain in my back and legs and told the guards that I wanted medical attention. Towards evening, they took me to a doctor, along with another prisoner, a Pakistani named Hicaz, who had diarrhea and a swollen tongue and was feeling weak. The doctor, an Iraqi, gave him a shot of penicillin and offered me some antibiotics. If nothing else, I thought, the antibiotics would provide some protection from whatever might be in the water at this camp.

There were only two toilets for all the prisoners, located at the outer edge of the camp and guarded by soldiers. They were filthy and the lines to use them were long. People who only had to urinate did it in the open field. When some of the

Indian prisoners dropped their pants to defecate in the field, the Iraqi soldiers stopped them and ordered them into the lines for the toilets. The Indians complained loudly and the soldiers yelled back in Arabic and waved their guns. As the arguing went on, neither side understanding the other, one man could wait no longer. He squatted down right then and there.

Later, we discussed why the Iraqis were holding so many foreigners - the hundreds of Asians, for example, who were in this camp. One possibility, we thought, was that Iraq wanted to remove foreigners from Kuwait as an act of intimidation and replace them with its own people.

Another theory was that by detaining the foreigners, the Iraqis would be able to delay or block any attempts by the United Nations to take action against Iraq for invading Kuwait. Imprisoned foreigners could be used as bargaining chips, to pressure their governments and discourage them from taking political, economic, or military action against Iraq. We even considered the specific cases of each of the countries represented in camp - how Iraq could benefit from holding, for example, Pakistanis, Sri Lankans, or Turks.

The most frightening scenario was that Iraq would utilize the foreigners it held as "human shields," moving them to strategic sites in Iraq to keep outside forces from bombing them from the air. This idea initially seemed to be farfetched, but the truth was that we could really only guess at Iraq's intentions.

In the evening disputes broke out among prisoners over places to sleep and positions in the line for water. The tension and the uncertainty was putting many of the prisoners increasingly on edge, while others seemed to be falling into despair. To overcome this, many of the prisoners began telling the stories of their capture, some funny, some sad, sharing their experiences and their fears. This not only helped to pass the time, but gave the prisoners a sense of commonality, a feeling that we were all in this together.

One story was particularly dramatic. An Indian man said he had been living in Kuwait with his family. He had had to take his wife to the hospital for an operation, and had left his six- and seven-year-old children at home. About two hours later, he was told that the operation had been a success and so he left to return home. Before he got there he was abducted by Iraqi soldiers and transported to Iraq. He was half crazy with worry about his wife and his children. Many in our group were anxious about their families. But even though we were completely cut off, at least we knew our loved ones were relatively safe back in Turkey. The Indian man's story put some things into perspective. But at the same time it underlined the insanity of our situation.

We had agreed that Husnu would be the one responsible for regularly listening to the radio for news of the world. He was the most proficient at English and the most skilled at distilling what he heard from the various broadcasts into a concise briefing for the rest of us. Soon we were calling him "32nd Day," after a Turkish news program known for its accurate and succinct coverage of global events.

So as not to be detected, Husnu would sit in a corner of the room with a blanket over his head and use a tiny set of earphones. The Iraqi guards would come by periodically on their rounds and peer inside the rooms. So when Husnu would go inside for the news on the hour, we would stand in the doorway and in front of the broken window to provide cover. When the news programs were over, Husnu would come outside and we'd gather around him to hear his report.

The prison rooms were so cramped, we were forced to sleep outdoors that night. Even so, there was little space among the hundreds of others to put down our blankets. As we lay down all pushed together, some of the other prisoners who had been there a few days said food would be brought in the morning, maybe rice, and soldiers would use shovels to dump it onto the trays we had seen. Meanwhile, we had saved a few morsels of that hard, black bread to get us through the night.

I woke up at some point and discovered Ahmet Nakiboglu soaking our T-shirts and placing them over the mouth of our little steel water barrel. He was soaking them over and over and as they were dried dry by the constantly blowing hot wind, it cooled the water by the technique of evaporation. "I made a chiller," he said. "Can I offer you some cold water?"

He gave me a taste and it was quite cool. Throughout the night he kept wetting the shirts and chilling water for us to drink. In the midst of this chaos, such simple ingenuity gave us hope and helped keep us sane. It was our first night inside a prison. We were reconciling ourselves to the idea that this would not end as soon as we had hoped, and we tried to prepare ourselves. It was a dispiriting thought, yet somehow we were gathering the strength and fortitude to carry on. By now, we even seemed to be getting used to sleeping on bare ground.

Sunday, August 5th, 1990

I awakened around 5:30 am, stood up and looked around. In the yard between the two lines of buildings, there must have been six hundred people sleeping. Some had blankets to lie on, others had nothing. Some slept on the cement and others on the dirt. It looked as if people had been tossed about topsy-turvy, with one person's head resting on someone else's foot, a leg thrown over someone's back, a few knees bent in the air. As I watched, bodies and limbs would shift, trying to find some minimal comfort. I saw someone's hand push a foot off his head and heard someone groan. A few moments later, after sleep had resumed, the same foot managed somehow to end up resting again on the same head.

As others started to rise, they had to tip-toe their way over and through those who were still sleeping to reconnect with their nationality groups. At one glance, I could take in a whole array of nations. Some were speaking to each other in low voices in assorted languages. Everyone's clothes were muddy and stained. The ones who had been here the longest were pale and weak, staring at their hands or off into space.

The sun began to come up. The ground had hardly cooled overnight. The heat was so embedded in the earth that it seemed to have baked our bodies.

As the rest of our group awakened, I noticed that the construction workers were continuing to treat the engineers with the same respect and deference they would show during our regular working lives. Still, I could occasionally detect a slight grin beneath their mustaches as they observed us, their superiors, with cloths all filthy, having to adjust like everyone else to these awful conditions. Maybe they were a bit amused at the way dire circumstances could erase the lines of status. Nonetheless, we all shared an anger toward the Kuwaiti government, because Kuwait had misread Iraq's intentions and, then, when the invasion had come, proved to be completely incapable of protecting anyone caught in the crossfire.

Among our group there was a great desire to hear the views of other nationalities - about Kuwait, about the invasion, about what had happened to each other and about what might happen next. I especially wanted to hear what the Kuwaiti soldiers had to say. That morning I managed to speak with one of the Kuwaiti army officers. "How did it happen?" I asked him. "Was there any resistance? What were you doing at the time?"

To my surprise, he said, "To tell you the truth, we were sitting in our room. The door opened and the Iraqis just walked in."

I was stunned. "But wasn't it the army's job to know if they would be coming, and where they would be coming from and when?" I asked. "Didn't you have some type of surveillance system or intelligence service monitoring the situation. Isn't an army supposed to be prepared for such contingencies?"

"Honestly, to observe and gather information is not our job," he responded. "We are trained for fighting. We never received word that the Iraqis were invading. You should be asking those who were responsible for intelligence."

I related what the officer had told me to our group and to members of other nationality groups. Everyone in the camp seemed to agree that the Kuwaiti government, unable to protect its own nation, was in large part responsible for our being here in this situation. Some people asked how the Kuwaitis could not have been prepared, especially after the Iraqi army had begun to amass along the border.

There appeared to be resentment among many of the prisoners because of Kuwait's great wealth. Did the Kuwaitis believe that their luxury and privilege somehow made them immune to aggression, some asked. It seemed to me that many of the prisoners needed to hold someone responsible for our predicament. Some had long admired Kuwait, for its social system, for the way it was organized, and for its economy. But the admiration had turned to anger. Most of the prisoners now seemed to think that a government that could not carry out basic self-defense should not even be considered a state.

Meanwhile, some of the Iraqi officers told us that we might have to stay only for a few days, as "guests." But we no longer believed such statements. It was now clear that we had been lied to from the very first day. We decided to ask for another meeting with the camp commander and gave a note to the guards with our request. They took the note but did nothing.

Suddenly, there was a stir in the camp and many of the prisoners began moving toward the area where the food trucks usually parked. Some were excited, almost desperate, at the thought of food and it looked like there might be a disturbance. Our group hung back, as did the Chinese, waiting to see what would happen.

But there wasn't to be any food. An Iraqi soldier approached and told us all to gather our belongings: we were leaving. I put what I had - a collared shirt, a T-shirt and a pair of underpants - into my small nylon bag and walked with the others to the square where we had been processed on arrival. The announcement seemed to give everyone a lift. But where would they take us now?

In the square they counted us one by one and checked our names on their lists. They lined us up in rows of four and five and ordered us to sit on the ground. After a while, we were we boarded by nationality onto buses. Sitting in the front as usual, I could see that the members of our group were tense with anticipation, no-one saying anything, no-one wanting even to speculate what would happen next.

Soon we were traveling through the streets of Basra and now everyone seemed to be calling out at once. As the bus turned at one intersection, someone cried, "Oh no, we are going in the direction of Baghdad." Down another street and somebody else said, "We're okay, we're heading towards Kuwait City." When we passed by a river port, I thought of the possibility they would put us on boats, but the convoy of buses kept on going.

Finally, we arrived at a train station and parked. As we waited, our bus - filled with our entire group and without air-conditioning - became like an oven. It was the worst in the back. We had brought our water barrel with us and kept sending cups to those seated in the rear. I heard someone say, "I'm going to faint." It was Mehmet Cetinkoprulu. He was brought to the front and seated by the open door. He was drenched in sweat and barely conscious. Then others started coming forward, weak and wobbly. We had been waiting nearly two hours.

Soon we heard shouts from the other buses as prisoners jumped out, seeking relief. Our group got out as well, but it was really no better in the sun. The hopes we had had when we left the prison camp seemed to be dying in the heat of Basra.

The next thing we knew, soldiers were running around trying to herd us into a long single line. Then I was approached by the commander of the camp we had just departed from. He addressed me as "Mustesar" - literally, Undersecretary - acknowledging me as the person in charge. He apologized, saying, "Inshallah" (with Allah's permission), "this will end very soon. Sometimes things happen this way during war." He added, "I have reserved a very good place for you on the train."

"Where is the train going?" I asked him.

"Baghdad," he said.

I informed the members of our group. They seemed stunned and deflated all at once.

The commander walked me away from the group, apologizing over and over again, trying to appease me, saying that during wartime some things could not be helped.

Finally, we were taken onto the train and were quite surprised to find that it had cold running water, clean toilets and even sleeping compartments. The commander escorted me to a compartment designed for four people. He said that I would have it all to myself. I declined and said that I would be sharing it with my colleagues. "Very well," he said.

I was joined by Osman, Ozer and Mehmet Cetinkoprulu. The other members of our group settled into nearby compartments, all of us in the same car.

The train was soon traveling north toward Baghdad, moving along at a high speed. Through the windows, we could see other trains going in the opposite direction towards Basra, loaded with tanks, artillery and troops. We decided that Iraq, in reality, was one huge military installation. Somebody said, "I don't think there is an Iraqi government. We should just call it the United Army of Iraq."

Even though we still had no idea what was happening, the unexpected comfort of the train made many of us optimistic. It was the first chance to shave in days and both engineers and construction workers were clowning around in the aisles. Some of us reminded them that we should not get our hopes too high. We should stay calm.

Still, some wanted to believe that the Iraqis would not have put us on such a nice train unless they intended to release us in Baghdad. Others warned that it could just be the calm before the storm. The more pessimistic views seemed to be reinforced by the Iraqi soldiers who kept checking on us through the Venetian blinds on the windows facing the aisle that ran the length of the cars.

The train passed through long stretches of wide, empty terrain. The soil seemed fertile, but it was dried out and cracked by the sun. As engineers, we imagined how an irrigation system could be installed and concluded that if the Saddam Hussein regime had spent its resources on agriculture rather than armaments, this area could be brought to bloom.

Later the train rolled past fields of dates, almost like forests - they were so extensive. The dates were ripe and golden yellow and occasionally we could see idyllic houses nestled among the trees. It was along this picturesque stretch that we remembered we were in Mesopotamia, the cradle of civilization. Ever since I had read history in school, I had wanted to see this. It was ironic, to say the least, that I was finally doing so in the custody of a dictator who seemed determined to see civilization destroyed.

Early in the afternoon, having traveled for hours, we stopped at a station. We could see women carrying bread and other items onto the train. Soon after we left the station, the food was brought around - meatballs, bread and fruit juice. The commander himself came to our compartment to offer us some grapes. Again, he apologized for the "inconvenience."

When he was gone, I said to my colleagues that there had to be something else behind all these apologies, that we needed to remain wary and vigilant. The hope was that after all this courteous treatment everyone would be taken to their respective embassies in Baghdad and released. As if to support that theory, the commander returned with a number of soldiers and ordered them to put fresh linen on the beds in our compartment.

Along the way, we read the names of the stations we passed and tracked them on the map that Taner had brought along. Someone pointed out that as we approached Baghdad the train would come to a junction and either continue north toward Karbala and Baghdad, or branch off toward the east and Iran.

Again, there was fear that we would end up in one of the POW camps Iraq had used for Iranian prisoners in the 1980s. We held our breath when we came to the junction and were greatly relieved when the train proceeded north.

The train pulled into Baghdad just as the sun was setting. Iraqi soldiers lined us up in the aisle of the car, where we waited for some time before exiting. The station was bustling with people, all going about their business as usual, no-one paying us any attention.

Again the prisoners were stuffed into an array of buses. I sat in the front again, with the water barrel next to me and Ozer sitting on top of it. I noticed a nearby bus terminal, separated from the train station by only a few rail tracks. The terminal was busy and people were walking back and forth across the tracks to the station. Beyond the terminal there seemed to be a thoroughfare of some sort. It was then that I noticed the soldiers guarding our vehicle were momentarily distracted. How hard would it be just to stroll across the tracks, into the bus terminal and out the other side, into the city streets?

Later on, my colleagues admitted they had thought the same thing. However, I had believed from the beginning that it would be irresponsible to try to escape on my own. If something had gone wrong, it would have jeopardized the entire group. So I had decided that I would not attempt it without consulting everyone. Plus, here in Baghdad, there was still the hope of being taken to our embassy and released.

As we were waiting, numerous Iraqi military vehicles with sirens blaring pulled alongside the line of buses. When the buses finally started moving, the military vehicles joined the procession, broadcasting announcements in Arabic over loud speakers. Cars with sirens and flashing lights pulled out ahead and cleared the way.

Mehmet Cetinkoprulu knew the streets of Baghdad from the three years he had lived there working on the Kutlutas project in the 1980s. So with every turn he was trying to determine what our destination might be. At one point he exclaimed, "Oh, my God, I think we're heading for the infamous Al-Ambar military base." What do you mean infamous, we asked.

Mehmet explained that Al-Ambar was one of the worst places in Iraq, where Iranian POWs and enemies of the government were taken during the war. The belief was that no prisoner who went in, came out. The group became very quiet. Mehmet said that when he lived in Baghdad there were all kinds of horrible stories and rumors about the place - starvation, torture, executions. Many Iraqis were drawn to Al-Ambar, as if to a horror movie, he said. Once even he had approached the place out of grim curiosity. But the guards would never let anybody get near.

Meanwhile, most of the people we passed on the streets did not seem to know or care what this procession of vehicles was all about. Eventually, we were able to decipher that the loudspeakers were telling the people of Baghdad that we were important prisoners. But I could see from the expressions on their faces that they did not grasp who we were or why we were being transported through the streets in such a spectacular way. On a few occasions, people applauded as we passed by, while every now and then a woman would appear to look at us with pity.

As this lurid parade continued through the city, our hopes fell yet again. It was obvious we were not being taken to our embassies. Some of us had held out hope that Saddam Hussein would realize the benefit of releasing us: it would make him appear a statesman, respectful of the rights of civilians. That, of course, was a pipe dream.

As we found ourselves circling back around by the bus station, we realized the regime had simply been putting us on display, like prizes, for all to see. But now the show was over. After a while, the procession of vehicles entered a base through a gate with "Iraqi Military Police" printed in bold letters. The soldiers on duty inside seemed highly disciplined and the base was orderly. At least it wasn't Al-Ambar.

We drove down a long road lined with trees that came to an end at a large square. We were ordered out of the buses, separated by nationality and arranged in rows of five. Once assembled, we appeared now to number nearly a thousand. Some of us half expected Saddam Hussein himself to arrive with television crews to show off his human trophies.

Sitting on a chair in one corner of the square was a high ranking military officer, who appeared to be the commander of this facility. He looked solid, strong. We could see an eagle and three stars on his epaulets and we figured he was a general. There were about two dozen other officers around him and soldiers with machine guns all over the place.

I was sitting on our water barrel while the rest of our group sat on the ground with their legs crossed. One of the soldiers approached us and asked for the "Undersecretary." Everyone pointed at me. The soldier said that his commander wished to speak with me, so I went along. The commander stood up and shook my hand politely and offered me a chair. He was extremely cordial and respectful.

I asked him why we had been brought to this base. What were their intentions? Rather than answer, he asked me my profession.

I told him that I was chairman of a Turkish firm formed by a number of Turkish companies and the Turkish government, that I had been to Iraq many times, that I had come on formal visits with Turkish ministers, and that I had attended business conferences in Baghdad. I said that I could neither understand nor tolerate the way we had been abducted and brought here from Kuwait and that it would surely create ill will against Iraq in Turkey, especially since the Turkish people had supported Iraq during its war with Iran. I said that if Iraq was thinking of using us as bargaining chips, the Turkish people wouldn't stand for it. I reminded him that Turkey was a democratic country, and that its government could not easily make decisions against public opinion. To use us has hostages, I said, would do Iraq more harm than good.

When he did not respond, I asked him how much longer we would be held. "For a very short time," he said. "We are really very sorry. These kinds of mistakes happen during times of war. Please bear with us for a few days."

We had arrived in Baghdad with the hope of being released. When he said a few days, it sounded like a few years. Noticing my anger and dismay, he said, "You have to understand, our American friends are causing us difficulties."

I was infuriated by the suggestion that I would somehow be assuaged because Iraq's invasion of Kuwait was causing problems for the Iraqi regime. At the same time, my sixth sense told me that we had in fact become pawns - that things would get worse before they got better.

He stood and thanked me. We shook hands and I was escorted back to our group. Everyone was anxious to hear what had been said. I said that it didn't look good and watched as my friends and colleagues sagged in disappointment. Many seemed to withdraw into their own thoughts, worried and discouraged. I told them the commander had said we would probably have to stay there for a couple of days, but that it was still unclear. When I told them about his statement regarding problems with the Americans, everyone concluded that the Iraqis must be using us as a deterrent against an American attack.

As we continued to mull over our situation, more hostages were being brought in. Soldiers lined them up, called out names and counted each arriving group. Sometimes they would count and recount the same group a number of times, huddle among themselves gesturing and speaking in Arabic, and then count them all over again. I cannot remember how many times our group was counted.

The various groups were then marched around the camp. At first, it appeared that we might be put on the buses again. But eventually we stopped in front of an imposing building and soldiers opened a steel door. We were ordered to enter, single file, and found ourselves in a long hallway, in water up to our ankles. At the end of the hallway were more soldiers. We turned to the right, went about fifty meters, passed through another steel door and found ourselves inside a block of single-story buildings with barbed wire strung along their roofs. Iron doors, barbed wire - the people in my group had never even stood before a judge, let alone gone to jail. Now we were in one of Saddam Hussein's prisons and a deep fear, stark and unadulterated, set in among us all.

Next we passed through a small door with iron bars into a courtyard about twenty-five meters long and ten meters wide. The first thing we noticed was the horrible stench of excrement and urine. Near the door there was a sink, cloudy water flowing incessantly from a faucet and spilling from the basin onto the floor. Toilet stalls stood in a pond of fetid water along one of the walls and, as we discovered, only two of them were functional. The scum in the gutter that ran along one side the courtyard was so oddly colored that we doubted the gutter had ever been cleaned.

A half hour passed, then an hour, and we remained there, gagging on the putrid air, the soldiers staring at us without a word. My watch now read two o'clock in the morning. There were maybe one hundred and fifty of us in this courtyard. Some were so overcome with exhaustion that they lowered themselves onto the wet and stinking floor and nodded off to sleep.

I was not tired. Or if I was, I was too agitated to sleep. Amazingly, our construction workers had managed to hold on to our water barrel and again I used it for a seat. I leaned back and looked up at the sky, which on this night seemed very far away. I surveyed the sleeping bodies wedged together on the wet floor and it seemed like I was in an open can of sardines.

I could not sit still for long and began stepping around sleeping bodies to stretch my legs. An overweight young man with a withered arm and a severe limp also was still awake. He spoke English and told me that he was a Palestinian from Jordan who had been working for some type of company in Kuwait. I asked him how he had ended up with us. He said he did not know, that he was arrested without explanation. He seemed extremely uncomfortable. Putting someone so disabled through this ordeal seemed to me the height of cruelty. I offered him the barrel to sit on and he seemed to find it comfortable enough to doze off for a while. But later, he moved over near the gutter, the only place left where he could stretch out a little, and placed his head on the cement ledge next to the stream of waste that was flowing by.

Later we were startled by the racket of people banging their fists and feet against the iron door from inside the building. Some of us had been talking quite loudly, so at first I thought they were banging on the door to get is to quiet down. The thought of someone being tortured also crossed my mind. But I would soon find out the real reason. For we would be jammed into those buildings too, and once locked in, if you needed to use the bathroom you had to bang on the door until the soldiers let you out.

I sat back down on the barrel and managed to catch a few moments of sleep. Just before sunrise, I bathed to the extent it was possible using the broken sink. The heat was already rising, making the stench that much worse.

Monday, August 6th, 1990

At about 6 am, the Iraqi guards opened the steel door that had been pounded and kicked during the night and a mob of prisoners burst through, desperate to use the facilities. They had been denied access the entire night.

Soon after dawn, swarms of flies descended upon the courtyard. With the sun rising, we again had to figure out a way to protect ourselves. By late morning, human skin would burn in a matter of minutes. We managed to negotiate with some of the prisoners inside the buildings for the use of some of their blankets, which we fashioned into a tent-like cover connected to one of the walls, similar to the one we had set up in the camp in Basra.

Then we cleaned out the area and tried to make ourselves comfortable in this little patch of shade. Developing a plan and carrying it out, even for something as simple as putting up a tent, seemed to boost the morale of our group as we tried to overcome the shock of being deposited in this awful place.

An Iraqi soldier came into the courtyard, approached our group and asked for "the Undersecretary." We were now used to the Iraqis using that term to mean leader or chief. He said that he had orders from his commander that I was to have anything I wanted. At first we laughed. Osman said that I should order two soft-boiled eggs. We wondered what was going on.

The soldier was not amused. I asked him if he would bring us some ice and some more blankets. He left and, much to our surprise, returned shortly with what I had asked for. Later, he brought us a pile of soggy rice that had been dumped onto one of those two-handled, metal trays that looked like they had once been part of a tea service. There was also some of that black bread we had first encountered in Basra - flat, round buns almost too hard to chew. A less appetizing meal would be hard to imagine, but we were still famished from the previous day so we ate our fill.

A hush came over the courtyard when an Iraqi officer walked in. He looked around until he saw our group, then came over and told me that his commander wanted to see me. When I insisted that the other engineers accompany me, he hesitated but finally agreed. When the officer told us to take our personal belongings, our construction workers stirred, wondering if we were going to be released, leaving them behind. But then he told them to come along as well, raising hopes that we would all be let out together.

So we went back through the metal doors, past the armed guards, single-file through the flooded hallway and out into the well-kept grounds around the administration buildings. The engineers and myself were ordered into a single-story structure and into what appeared to be a conference room with a long table and about two dozen chairs. We were offered cold water. The commanding officer entered and read our names one by one from a sheet of paper. He asked each one of us who we were and why we had been in Kuwait.

The engineers were then put into a side room with sagging armchairs and a television set. While we watched television, our workers were brought into the conference room and questioned. There were two other foreigners in the television room, one of them a European who spoke English and said he worked for a Kuwaiti telephone company. He had been captured in Kuwait too.

Iraqi television was broadcasting nothing but Saddam Hussein. He was here, there and everywhere, with people praising him and singing songs to him. We wondered whether the Iraqi people actually paid attention to this sort of thing on their televisions. It was not long before a number of us nodded off to sleep. We could overhear our workers being interrogated in the next room and a few of us still held out the hope that our continuing detention was the result of administrative problems, a question of paperwork, too much bureaucracy.

When the questioning of the workers was completed, we were informed by one of the officers that we were to be moved to a different part of the compound. When we asked about being released, he said, "Soon."

We were led around the grounds for a while, then herded back in the direction of the courtyard. It was like being kicked in the chest. The roller coaster was on the downswing again. It seemed that part of their strategy was to wear us down mentally as well as physically.

As so we retraced our path again, through the same foul water in the dank hallway and through sets of metal doors. But this time, they had put us into one of the prison buildings off the stinking courtyard. There were hundreds of men crammed into this room. We asked to be returned to the courtyard, but were told that was not possible.

As our eyes adjusted to the shadows, we could see that the prisoners were packed in so tight that many had to remain standing. Most were shirtless in the suffocating heat. We heard the heavy door slam shut behind us. Any hopes we may have been holding onto were gone - we were prisoners of war.

It took us a long time to find a place for our group to squeeze in. The building was actually a metal shed. It was about forty meters long and twenty-five meters wide, with a space of about three and a half meters, floor to ceiling. The windows were small, with vertical iron bars, and were cut high in the walls, up near the ceiling.

Everyone inside was glistening with sweat. Some had towels, undershirts and torn pant legs wrapped around their heads. There was a constant hum of voices, punctuated by coughs and the occasional shout. With a bit more time to look around, I estimated there were around seven hundred prisoners, which would mean a little more than one square meter for each of us. Later we would find out that there was a similar shed on the other side of the courtyard that was holding at least as many prisoners. That meant there were possibly as many as fifteen hundred people being held just in the area of this courtyard.

Unsurprisingly, I could also see that people were generally congregating by nationality - which is what we did, carving out a space, after some jostling and negotiating with other groups, in a corner near the main door. We brushed the floor as clean as we could, put down some stray cardboard we found and laid out some of our blankets.

We stacked all our belongings against the wall in such a way that it created a semblance of an enclosure. Here Husnu, with a blanket over his head, could continue to monitor the news broadcasts. We kept the radio secret from the other prisoners, because we could not risk having the guards find out about it. The radio was a lifeline, the oxygen hose through which we breathed to stay alive.

By now Husnu knew when all the most important news programs were aired, particularly on the BBC. Not much had changed since we'd been taken out of Iraq. The U.S. was continuing to lead a further military buildup in the region and Saddam Hussein was remaining defiant. The only thing that seemed to be increasing was the tension. There were not many scenarios we could envision for ourselves other than getting bombed by U.S. forces from the air, being executed by the Iraqi regime, being held indefinitely, or being freed. The news that Husnu relayed to us suggested that the last possibility was the least likely.

One thing that seemed certain was that Saddam Hussein remained firmly entrenched in power and, short of a mass popular revolution, would probably remain so. And that meant this crisis could go on indefinitely.

A question we kept coming back to was, why were the Iraqis holding Turkish prisoners, and what leverage might that give the Saddam Hussein regime. One possibility was that they planned to use us as bargaining chips to prevent Turkey from shutting down the oil pipeline that runs from Iraq through Turkey. Another was that they wanted to discourage Turkey from joining any international embargo against Iraq. We were not convinced, though, that our being held would have much influence on the Turkish government. We believed that Turkey would not submit to Iraqi blackmail and would join an embargo or close the pipeline if that was the position of the international community. We felt that Iraq might be holding us for other reasons.

The latest news from the radio was that the United States was going to deploy troops in Saudi Arabia. Having seen the Iraqi forces roll through Kuwait, we had considered the possibility that they might continue on into Saudi Arabia. Saudi Arabia meant the Aramco oil company, and Aramco meant the U.S. So, obviously, America would protect its interests there.

Another scenario that crossed our minds was that Saudi Arabia and the United Arab Emirates, with the help of the CIA and the KGB, would spend millions of dollars trying to incite a revolution against Saddam Hussein.

Our group tried to envision what might happen next. Some thought that Saddam Hussein, believing that he was going to be overthrown or killed, would shoot all the hostages as a final act of vengeance. Others thought that even if Saddam gave such an order, the army would refuse to carry it out and would celebrate Saddam's downfall instead. With little to do other than contemplate our fate amidst this profound uncertainty, our imaginations ran wild, leaping from one scenario to the next.

We noticed there were hundreds of small holes in the walls of the shed, most of them at about eye level. We thought they might be bullet holes, evidence of executions of previous prisoners, lined up against the wall and shot. In some of the holes we found what appeared to be bullets or bullet fragments. Sections of the walls were newly painted, and we wonder if that was to cover up blood stains. Were we in some kind of slaughterhouse? We could not discount the possibility and the idea chilled us — even in the incredible heat.

On other sections of the walls, names had been scrawled, no doubt by prisoners who had been there before us. We wondered what had happened to them, whether they were still alive. We decided that we had better put our names on the wall, too. Rather than write them with a pen, we carved them, so that if the worst happened they would be more lasting and would not simply vanish under a coat of paint. Later on, someone would be able to see that we had been here, maybe even members of the TJV staff in Kuwait if they too were abducted and brought here.

Rumors buzzed among the prisoners that this facility had been used for Iranian POWs during the war. Given the disrepair and deterioration, it was obvious it had been in existence for some time. Toward one side there was a slightly elevated area, a platform with a one-inch ridge around it that functioned as a urinal. If you really had to go, and couldn't wait for the guards to hear you banging on the door and let you into the courtyard, then you used this little platform.

It was not enclosed, so you had to get used to standing up and urinating in full view of your seven hundred fellow prisoners. Some of the prisoners decided to make light of the situation by turning it into a performance.

One of them was a man from the Philippines whom I had met earlier out in the courtyard. He told me the Iraqi soldiers had confiscated his thirteen thousand dollar car in Kuwait and taken a diamond ring right off his finger. I later heard he worked for an oil-drilling company. When he stepped up onto the platform, a number of the prisoners began to applaud. He turned and waved his member in response and the applause turned into cheering. Finally, just about everyone was laughing and carrying on as if they were at some burlesque show. Every now and then, someone else would step up to take a turn.

Even when there was no performance going on, there was always a loud murmur in the room, as all the various groups traded stories and, like us, tried to figure out what was going to happen next. With so many people in such a small space, the buzz would only begin to die down around midnight as people started to fall asleep.

Lunch was the same soggy rice slopped onto those two-handled trays. Guards brought them to the door and invariably there was jostling and yelling as everyone tried to get their share. Thankfully, our workers were quite agile in dealing with the situation. Some of the prisoners were not and were left out.

A Pakistani man told us he had been unable to get food for the past two meals, so we gave him some of ours. There was no bread this time. There were no spoons, either, so we ate with our fingers or improvised with scraps of paper or cardboard we had in our pockets.

Our workers were also skilled at plying the guards for ice and water. They figured out ways to carry water in their caps. Their ingenuity throughout this ordeal made it easier for all of us in the group.

There were also occasional fights, usually over a blanket or for space on the floor - precious commodities under these conditions. But they didn't last long and there was no real harm inflicted, as others always quickly stepped in to calm things down. Meanwhile, it was almost impossible to shave; beards were growing on nearly every face. People hung their shirts around their necks like towels or tied them into turbans to absorb the sweat.

That night, when Husnu came out from under his blanket to give us a review of what was being reported on the radio, he told us that Iraq was said to be moving military units towards Saudi Arabia, which meant it was preparing for a possible attack. For the time being, the U.S. was advocating only an economic embargo against Iraq, but it was expected to come to the Saudis' defense if Iraq invaded. It was also reported that fifteen countries had now joined the U.S. in boycotting Iraqi oil.

Iraq, meanwhile, claimed that it was moving out of Kuwait. The U.S. said that Iraq was lying, that Baghdad was repeatedly broadcasting the same video footage of an Iraqi ship leaving a Kuwaiti port and that the ship had in fact returned to Kuwait, which Washington said it had confirmed through satellite surveillance.

The BBC reported that Saddam Hussein was issuing weapons to civilian members of his Baath Party, possibly because he was afraid of elements within his own military and the possibility of an army rebellion.

It was also reported that Iraq had shut down one of the two pipelines into Turkey, a response to the oil boycott. We thought that Iraq must have consulted with Turkey before doing this.

Finally, there were reports from Kuwait that at least three and possibly more members of the ruling Al-Sabah family had been hanged by Iraqi occupation forces.

We spent a long time considering the possible implications of these new developments, and found little reason for optimism. It was only our second night inside this horrendous place, but we knew that we had to prepare ourselves for an indefinite stay.

As the hours wore on, a number of new prisoners arrived, Chinese, British, Russian, Hungarian and Greek. Somehow they managed to squeeze into these already hellishly cramped quarters. And they would soon learn, as well, about the night-long pounding on the metal door as people begged the guards for water or a chance to use a toilet.

Tuesday, August 7th, 1990

I woke early and saw that nearly everyone else was still asleep. As the others began to rise, soldiers came and began moving prisoners a few at a time into the courtyard, where some food and water were handed out. Meanwhile, lines formed on the other side of the courtyard for the only two useable toilets - two toilets for the thousand or more people in the sheds around the courtyard. Inevitably, tempers flared. As the hours passed, the smell only became worse. We decided that perhaps it was better that our group had been moved into a shed.

Following the chaos of the morning in the courtyard, and after we were put back inside, we noticed that Husnu seemed to be missing. He had been quiet since his last radio report the night before and we wondered if he had somehow tried to slip away. It was a form of wishful thinking, because we all harbored thoughts of escape, dreaming of somehow getting away to send word to our families. The more we thought about how them, the more we wanted to let them know we were alive.

I kept thinking of my children and the pain they must be feeling not knowing what had happened to me. I thought that if I were in their place, that if they were the ones who were missing, the fear and the worry would have been unbearable. And I knew that each one of my colleagues felt the same way.

Some were certain that their parents had become ill or even died because of the worry. For us all, it was more painful and upsetting to think of our families and their health than it was to endure the conditions in this prison.

As these thoughts were racing through our minds, Husnu finally returned. He told us that he gone very early into the courtyard and had met some of the European prisoners. He had then gone with them to the third and smaller shed where they were being held. He joked that the Turkish group should be there, too, but that even Saddam Hussein did not perceive us as part of the European Community.

Husnu said that he had met the English and Hungarian groups, as well as the Japanese, who had been put in with the Europeans. The Japanese told him that Iraqi forces had removed them from the Sheraton in Kuwait City by telling them that the hotel was a potential bombing target and that for their own safety they would be brought to a similar quality hotel. Instead, they were abducted and taken into Iraq. They called this hell hole we shared "Camp Sheraton." The Iraqi soldiers had told them it was not necessary to take any of their belongings. So, they had arrived here with virtually nothing and were sleeping on the bare floor.

The Hungarians were sailors who had been seized from their ship in the Kuwait City harbor. The captain had to keep interrupting their story because he kept crying. Many of his crew were heavyset and struggling in the heat. One of them, a young man with a beard, slept almost all of the time.

The previous day, the members of our group had been discussing our situation, going over all the possible outcomes and how we could prepare ourselves. Today, however, there was little conversation. Most of us seemed distant, looking inward, individually trying to come to terms with our plight. Someone would speak, but the others mostly would just nod and return to their own reflections. It made for a darker, more pessimistic atmosphere.

Husnu became better each day at absorbing the various radio news broadcasts and providing the rest of us with detailed updates. During the first round of morning news, it was reported that the United Nations had voted in favor of an economic embargo against Iraq. Still, neither Turkey nor Saudi Arabia had closed off the oil pipelines leading out of Iraq. This made us hopeful because the implication was that Iraq still had an incentive to maintain stable relations with both countries. And if Baghdad wanted to stay on the good side of Turkey, it might not want to hold us too long.

Meanwhile, the U.S. Navy continued its buildup in the Gulf, while a U.S. assistant secretary of state was in Baghdad holding meetings with Iraqi officials. Additional naval vessels were being sent by the Soviet Union, Britain and other European countries. Upcoming diplomatic activity was said to include a visit by U.S. Secretary of State James Baker to Turkey, while his assistant would travel from Iraq to Saudi Arabia. For his part, Saddam Hussein said that Saudi Arabia was Iraq's friend, even as Iraqi military units continued to move south toward the Saudi border with Kuwait.

There was one report that said that Iraq was holding American and German hostages in a hotel, to which Taner commented, "But nobody knows what a comfortable hotel we are in here."

The most forceful and angry person on the international scene seemed to be Margaret Thatcher. She called for military action against Saddam Hussein that would "turn Iraq upside down." But although she was angry about the English hostages, she must not have been too concerned about them personally because she wanted to crush Iraq immediately. We joked that of all the players in this crisis, she was the only real man. We agreed with her that there could be no resolution to the crisis unless the world got rid of Saddam, that his actions were not those of a rational human being.

Another report noted that fifteen members of the U.N. Security Council had supported the embargo against Iraq, with Cuba and Yemen abstaining. It was agreed that the economic embargo would remain in place until Iraq had removed all its military forces from Iraq and the Kuwaiti government had been reinstated. That made Ahmet Nakiboglu pessimistic: he said, "There! Until that happens, we're sure to be kept here."

Husnu said that while he had been in the smaller shed that morning, the Europeans had told him that one of the Russian prisoners had claimed to be a diplomat. He had screamed and yelled until he was allowed to explain who he was to Iraqi officers, after which his embassy was contacted and he was released. Hearing that, we decided that we would try to see the commanding officer again and make some noise ourselves.

Just then shouting broke out. A Bangladeshi had walked through our area trailing some kind of dirt from his shoes and one of our group had become angry. The two men moved towards each other and compatriots of each group stood up to provide support. There was a brief scuffle but calmer heads prevailed before it could turn into a real fight.

It was interesting to see people who did not share the same language arguing so intensely. For a moment both sides had been shouting at each other at the top of their lungs, with neither side able to understand a word. Moreover, the person who took the lead in cooling everybody off was a Pakistani man who spoke neither of the languages. In the end, everyone made up.

The incident made me ponder the complicated nature of human behavior, especially how it can change under different circumstances. Under dire conditions such as these, one could easily lose sight of the larger picture and end up in a fight that essentially was over nothing. Impulsive actions under pressure could lead to consequences that would affect someone for the rest of their life. On the other hand, there was the rational desire to cooperate, to work together for the benefit of everyone, as was evident when the Pakistani and others stepped in to get the situation under control before any lasting damage could be done.

The incident over, we discussed how we would approach the camp commander. It was decided that we would emphasize three points. First, that Turkey would not be inclined to close the pipelines to Iraq under normal conditions. But if Iraq continued to hold Turkish hostages, then Turkish public opinion would turn against Iraq. If that happened, the Turkish government would be under great pressure to stop Iraqi oil from flowing through Turkey. Second, we would say that the conditions in which we were being held were intolerable. And third, I had diplomatic status and they could not hold me under international law. Since my passport was in Kuwait, they would have to contact the Turkish embassy in Baghdad to confirm my status as a diplomat. If it achieved nothing else, the embassy would become aware of our situation.

It was now 9 am. From the hourly news broadcasts we learned that there were thirty American hostages, and that both the U.S. and British governments were pressing Iraq to free hostages of those nationalities. However, there were no reports of Turkish hostages, not even on Turkish radio. This angered us because it seemed the Turkish public, which would certainly have supported us, was not being properly informed. Osman said, "I will grab the president around the neck, this president who does not care about his own people." It seemed to us that the Turkish government was treating the hostage situation lightly, while American, British and German diplomats were all coming to Baghdad to pressure the Iraqi government to have their people released. This created a great deal of consternation within our group.

We decided it was time to make our case to the camp commander. On the back of one of my business cards, I wrote, "I request a meeting with the General." One of our workers who spoke some Arabic, Mehmet, handed the card to one of the guards. They told him that the commander was not present on the base; they would give him the card when he returned.

Life in these miserable quarters went on, our weariness and uneasiness increasing as the hours passed. The monotony was broken for a while when we conversed with some of the people who had worked for the Hyundai corporation in Kuwait. They had also been abducted by the Iraqi military, but because they were so many, about half of them had been released during the trip north, while the other half had ended up in this prison. We agreed that if this was some type of play, it would have to be a farce.

As the morning progressed, the prisoners packed into our shed were becoming more agitated and the first protests broke out. When an Iraqi soldier would appear, people would start shouting and chanting and banging on the door or the walls to demand better treatment, more water and food, better facilities.

Soon after, a group of Iraqi soldiers, including some officers, entered and began talking to the various national groups. It turned out that they wanted to have the food distributed in a more orderly way. They talked about ensuring that there would be at least one tray for every ten people.

Taner said, "Oh, no, if they're becoming so organized it means they must be planning to keep us for a long time."

The Pakistani man, whose name was Hijaz, disagreed, saying, "No. Some of the prisoners have not been able to get

81

any food and have gone hungry, so it necessary to organize so that everyone is able to eat at least a little food."

The next time they brought food, it was some watery lentil soup with the hard, black bread. The bread was floating in the soup. Some people tried to fish it out and in the process spilled soup on themselves. But our clothes were in such a filthy state already that it didn't really matter.

A prisoner from Sri Lanka walked by our group and said, "If you gave this stuff to a dog, he wouldn't eat it." Not many of the prisoners could stomach it. Everyone mostly chewed some bread and washed it down with water.

Meanwhile, Husnu updated the news. He said that Turkish radio was continuing to report on the American and British hostages but saying nothing about hostages from other nations. It was yet a further blow to our morale. Osman said that he would ask the Turkish ambassador in Baghdad and the Turkish government in Ankara for an explanation someday.

As I mentioned, the area occupied by our group was next to the metal door. Near the middle of the floor was a desert cooler, a primitive device that utilized water and sunlight to chill the air, similar to what Ahmet Nakiboglu had devised for us at the military camp where we were held in Basra. Occasionally some of us would go over to try to cool off, but it was usually too crowded: prisoners were eager to take advantage of what under the circumstances was a luxury.

Taner kept dwelling on the "What ifs...?" For example, he asked, "What if we had offered some money to that Iraqi officer who took us out of Kuwait? Maybe he would have taken us to our embassy instead."

Nobody thought that could have worked, because it was at night, and who was to say we could have gotten into the embassy at that time, anyway?

Then he asked, "I wonder if we could have escaped from the train?" He just couldn't leave it alone. It was apparent that grueling experience of captivity was starting to get to him.

Each hour seemed to pass more slowly than the previous one. If we did not find something to keep our minds busy, depression would begin to overwhelm us. All of us were used to active, non-stop lives and now we were reduced to little more than sleeping and eating.

So we started moving around, meeting with other hostages, hearing their stories, comparing them with ours. At one point we heard the tale of some Greek sailors. When the Iraqi forces had taken over their ship, they had taken all the sailors except the two who had their wives with them, apparently because women could not be brought to the hostage camps. One of the sailors who had been taken was waiting for his wife, who had just arrived at the airport in Kuwait when the invasion started. He was extremely worried because the Iraqis had brought him here and he had no idea what had happened to his wife.

It was noon and the guards had opened the door to the courtyard to give us a half-hour break. This would be repeated two or three times a day, to let the hostages wash and use one of the two toilets. Each time the door was opened, we felt both anxious and happy. We would be nervous because when the door opened, who knew what they might be planning to do with us next? Then happy because of the freedom - just because of getting out of our dark hole for a while. The sun, of course, was burning hot, so it would not be long before we had to come back inside.

We began to wonder what Saddam Hussein might do in the event of some crisis, such as a bombing of Iraq or a military invasion by the U.S. and other international forces. He could easily threaten to kill us all. And as far as we knew, he had never made threats that he wasn't willing to follow through.

Therefore we agreed that we needed to organize ourselves to be able to respond to such contingencies. For one thing, we needed to think about planning an escape in case things became really hot. We had to keep open the possibility that at least some of us would get out to tell the world what had happened, so that if any of us were executed, we would not have died in obscurity.

This was really the first time we had talked seriously about organizing ourselves and putting together a viable escape plan. The conversation began with Mehmet Cetinkoprulu, who said, "Saddam thinks of his hostages like chickens. He thinks he has the right to grill and eat them any time he likes." Ahmet Nakiboglu added, "That's why he's counting us twice a day, to make sure he's not missing any of his chickens."

That was the tone of our discussion - black humor laced with fear and dread and punctuated by dry, hollow laughter.

Osman said, "Usually the police don't arrive until after the murder has been committed. It's up to us to think for ourselves if we want to stay alive. Otherwise, if there is some type of rescue mission, by the time they got here it could be too late."

Ozer said that it would be a shame if we were executed by ignorant, third-echelon Iraqi soldiers who only followed orders out of fear of Saddam Hussein.

Osman pointed to the metal exit door that was barely wide enough for one person to squeeze through. Spreading his arms to take in the seven hundred prisoners in the shed, he said, "Can you imagine all these people in a panic trying to get out of this door at the same time? At least forty or fifty of them would die in the crush."

The loneliness and isolation were coming down upon us today. It was like being in the jungle, with no one to help us but ourselves. We had to make sure that at least one of us got out alive, for the sake of all our families, so that they would know what had happened here.

One of the scenarios for escape we envisioned was this: start by overwhelming the guard at the door inside and disarming him. Then call for the guards outside, pretending we needed water or something else and when they came, overwhelm and disarm them. Taking their weapons, we would leave the prison area and, once out in the compound, commandeer cars or other vehicles and speed out into the streets, using the weapons for cover. We would then go directly to the Turkish embassy.

We agreed that it would be best to divide ourselves into teams. Since there were thirty-two of us, we decided to form six or seven groups of four or five people, with one of the engineers heading each group.

Taner disagreed with the plan. He said, "What if one of us gets to the end of his rope, loses his judgment and impulsively starts to put the plan into action when it was not possible to carry it out? It would put everyone else in great jeopardy."

Although the other national groups did not understand our language, they could tell that we were in the middle of a very intense discussion, particularly as we were sitting in a circle, something we hadn't done before.

One thing we agreed on was the importance of having someone outside the shed, to open the door in the case of an emergency. I was the logical choice, because the commander had given orders that I be given special privileges as the "Undersecretary." I had objected at the time, because I did not want to be treated differently from my compatriots, nor had I wanted to be separated from them. But now it seemed like a good idea to take advantage of the offer.

I had Mehmet, our Arabic speaking worker, relay my request to the guards. A while later the door was opened and an Iraqi sergeant named Oman called for me to come out. He said I would be allowed in the courtyard and in another shed about seven meters away. It was single-story, too, but smaller, only about four meters by six inside. When I entered, it seemed the air was hotter and dirtier than in the larger shed. I counted about twenty people. They were the European and Japanese hostages that Husnu had met the day before.

I decided to risk telling them about our radio, asked them to keep it a secret and brought them up to date on developments since the invasion. They told me that many of them, particularly the Japanese, had been brought here from the Sheraton Hotel in Kuwait. They had been abducted right in front of the French ambassador to Iraq and the Spanish attaché, who were also held for a number of hours until they had proved they were diplomats. The French ambassador had written down the names of the Europeans taken from the hotel and read them to the world over the wireless radio at his embassy. Among those abducted at the hotel were ten Americans. Supposedly they were taken to Basra, but nothing had been heard about them since then.

I wrote down all the names, addresses and telephone numbers of the hostages in this shed. Before returning to the courtyard, I suggested to them that we should establish some way of communicating. With the radio we would be the first to hear about any declaration of war against Iraq or other important developments, but our group was in the other shed and usually locked in. The Europeans agreed that Saddam Hussein had probably taken hostages to use them as a deterrent against the possible bombing of Baghdad.

In turn, because the door to their shed was never locked, we would need them to open our door in case of an emergency. They could see across the courtyard to the door of our shed with the small, barred window. I told them that if there were an emergency and we had to have our door opened, we would put a drawing of a skull in that window. They all liked the idea in a morbid kind of way and agreed to watch for it.

Meanwhile, I wanted to know the various places where the guards were stationed, how many there were, where they came from and went to, and when they changed shifts. I consulted two of our workers, Mehmet, because he could speak the same language as the guards, and Ahmet, who had used his limited Arabic to become close enough to the guards to be allowed to sleep in the courtyard. I explained to them what we needed to know about the guards and asked them to see what they could find out, but without arousing suspicion.

I had been with the Europeans for about three hours. It was not a long time, really, but it was the first time I had been apart from our group. When I came inside our shed, they greeted me heartily. It felt good to be back among them.

There had been some interesting developments in my absence. The group had managed to get some ice from the guards, which meant we could chill water and store it in our water barrel. We were the only ones who had any kind of thermos, and taking it with us when we were taken from the Sabiya site in Kuwait was one of the smartest things we could have done. Often when prisoners became very thirsty in between breaks to the courtyard they would come to us.

At one point Ahmet Nakiboglu began angrily shouting at one of our workers and even got physical with him. "Is this the way you treat a person who asks for water?" he demanded of the worker. I saw that one of the Bangladeshi prisoners was standing nearby. The rest of workers quickly stood up and calmed the situation.

Ahmet told us that the Bangladeshi man had asked for water and been given some. Then he had come back a few times asking if he could have more. Our worker had become uneasy and yelled at the man, telling him not to ask for any more - that the water was not just for him. Ahmet said he had not known the whole story when he reprimanded our worker.

The next time the guards brought in rice, they gave everyone a cup, which meant people would no longer have to use their caps or berets to carry water from the courtyard. But it also made people anxious because everyone thought the glasses, along with the more organized distribution of food, were indications that we were going to be held for a long time.

That's the way it was for us: every change in routine, every bit of news that came from the radio, would be viewed through the lens of our captivity, examined from every angle to see how it might affect our status as hostages - how long we might be kept, what chances we had being released, whether we might become casualties in the geopolitical confrontation between Saddam Hussein and the international community.

The lead story on the radio news that afternoon was that Turkish President Turgut Ozal had announced that he would comply with all United Nations sanctions against Iraq, including the economic embargo.

There was also a report that Iraq had allowed some foreigners to leave Iraq, but only through Jordan. That gave us some hope, but there were few details and not really much to go on. Husnu predicted that if Jordan joined the embargo as well, the economic noose would become tight enough to spell the end of Saddam Hussein. Saddam, however, did not seem concerned. Reportedly, he said, "We are self sufficient. We are used to living in poverty."

That seemed true enough. We had seen how the Iraqi soldiers barely got by, and we also saw that the guards in this camp had to endure what were essentially the same conditions as us. They had to eat and drink what we did, plus they had the responsibility of being on guard without having received any salary in years. Even worse, they were not allowed to go home to visit their families.

It was also being reported that there were now three U.S. naval groups in the Gulf and nearly thirty thousand American troops. U.S. Secretary of State Baker was to be in Turkey tomorrow and from there he would go to Syria and Jordan.

The day before, during a break in the courtyard, I had encountered a young Iraqi officer talking to one of the Pakistani hostages who was a doctor. Iraqi forces had abducted him from a hospital, along with his male nurse and his driver, and brought him here specifically to attend to the prisoners. His family did not know what had happened to him. I had not seen him before. Taner said that he had seen him providing some medical care and advice to other hostages.

The Iraqi doctor I had encountered earlier also came into the courtyard. He spoke English relatively well. So I told him that I wanted to meet with the camp commander. I wrote another note on one of my cards and asked the doctor to give it to the general. This time I added that one of our engineers, Mehmet Dural Baran, was a cousin of Umit Mihat, the Iraqi Minister of Social Affairs. The Iraqi doctor was surprised by this and asked to speak with Mehmet Dural.

As usual Mehmet Dural was lying down inside. Although he was one of the best engineers anywhere when it came to steel, he had an unusually quiet nature. I don't think he spoke more than ten full sentences during our entire ordeal, and that is probably why I have not mentioned him up until now. I sent someone inside for him and a few minutes later he came out.

The Iraqi doctor asked Mehmet, "What is the nature of your relationship with Umit Mihat?" Mehmet pulled on his thin, curling mustache and told him, "The minister's mother and my father are brother and sister." The doctor said he would take my card to the camp commander.

Meanwhile, Taner continued to object to our escape plans and was disheartened by the tough stance Turkey was taking against Iraq. He was certain that it would delay our release and lessen our chances of getting out alive.

The heat remained oppressive and all of us were naked from the waist up. As I wrote down my notes, sweat dripped off the end of my nose. At the suggestion of Mehmet Cetinkoprulu, I cut the legs off my pants to turn them into shorts. Osman and Husnu did the same.

Around the middle of the afternoon the Voice of America reported that the U.S. economy was falling into recession. Rising oil prices were expected to push up bank interest rates and Washington was concerned. Ahmet Nakiboglu said, "So, this means that the Americans will try and reach some type of agreement with Saddam. That is what Saddam wants anyway."

I wondered why there had not been any mention in the news broadcasts of the hundreds, maybe thousands, of people from dozens of different nations who were now being held hostage in Baghdad.

Mehmet Cetinkoprulu said, "There are three, maybe as many as five, military bases in Baghdad. The Iraqis will position the foreigners at these bases to keep them from being bombed. It is obvious that such bases and camps will be bombed if the U.S. attacks."

Sedat, drawing on his experience as a colonel in the Turkish military, said, "Not necessarily - some are merely installations. A true military base would have tanks and anti-aircraft batteries and those would be more likely to be bombed."

We continued on like that for much of the afternoon, talking about nothing and everything.

Since early in the morning, Hercules transport planes had been taking off from somewhere near us. Out in the courtyard we could see their fat fuselages as they flew over our heads. We knew we must be very close to some type of air base.

Standing in the courtyard during a break, we considered escaping by climbing onto the roofs of the single-story sheds in which we were held. Taner said it wouldn't work because the roof was not open. I told him to stop being so pessimistic, that it only sapped our strength and undermined our morale.

As part of his Muslim faith, Ahmet Nakiboglu adhered to the schedule of praying five times a day. He had discovered that among the Indian group there was an Imam who held regular prayer sessions and had "a divine glow about his face." Ahmet had let it be known that he would like to pray under his guidance. When the Imam's followers came for Ahmet, he quickly performed a tayammum with his hands - a dry cleansing ritual performed when water is scarce or not immediately available - and went to join in the prayers.

Meanwhile, Osman was sleeping. At this point he seemed to be sleeping more than anyone in our group. He wore only the blue pajama bottoms he had cut off at the thighs to turn into shorts.

Mehmet Dural Baran was in pajamas, too, sitting in a relaxed way, almost lounging as if he were at home, and not commenting one way or another on any of the news from the radio. If someone asked him a direct question, he might answer, but in just a few words. Gently fingering his worry beads, he seemed at peace, patiently waiting and evidently prepared to accept whatever fate had in store for him.

Taner remained his usual pessimistic self and was continually anxious or nervous about something. If someone agreed with his bleak predictions, he would become even more agitated. He needed constant reassurance. I therefore read to him from the Koran and tried to explain that faith, as well as good and evil, is given to us by God, and that what people do and what comes to pass, our faith cannot change.

Ibrahim liked to play cards with the workers, who played frequently to pass the time. But whenever the engineers began a discussion - about news from the radio, politics, escape plans - jumping from one subject to the next and speculating on the future, the workers would gather around to listen.

On the hour, when it was time for the radio news, the workers would gather around Husnu to give him cover. Morale was generally high among most of the workers. A number of them were quite enthusiastic about trying to escape. Ahmet frequently came to me, saying, "Give me permission - I can disarm the guard by the door immediately. I can take control of the entire courtyard on my own and then overpower the other guards." He was very serious and said he wanted to be involved in any "mission operation" that we planned. Once he said, "These dirty soldiers can't give us orders. Who are they to keep us as hostages here? They can't give commands to us." He and other workers sometimes became very impatient with our wait-and-see strategy. A few times I thought Ahmet and some of the other workers just might go ahead and attack the guards on their own.

As expected, Ozer was carrying out a number of useful tasks. For example, he was in charge of overseeing and organizing the workers, especially as it related to water and food distribution. He was also ready to take a lead role in any plan to escape and even go after the Iraqi regime itself. He said, "I would sincerely love to take part in anything that will help overthrow Saddam. I would willingly spend a month in these conditions if it meant an end to Saddam."

Ahmet Nakiboglu continued to play his role as logistics manager, especially when it came to considering escape plans. He was constantly considering ways to get over the courtyard walls and the barbed wire or how we might construct some type of ladder.

We agreed that Mehmet Cetinkoprulu would think about how to divide us up into teams for any escape operation. He was donning his red and white polka dot, Palestinian-style scarf again and was shirtless, which he often preferred even before our capture. We kidded him, saying, "You started your suntan in Sabiya, buffed it in Basra and are having it polished in Baghdad. You could not have gotten a better tan than this."

At 5 pm, the BBC reported that Iraq had announced that Kuwaitis and some other foreign nationals were free to leave Iraq through Jordan. That made us very optimistic, hoping that the hostages would soon be told that they could leave as well.

It was notable that Iraq was allowing Kuwaitis to leave, but only into Jordan. We had previously heard that Iraqi soldiers had already begun to settle in Kuwait and were moving into confiscated or abandoned Kuwaiti houses. We believed that

Saddam Hussein's plan was eventually to have the Iraqis numerically dominate the population in Kuwait.

It was also reported that Turkish President Ozal had pledged to comply with the decisions of the United Nations but had not said whether Turkey would close the oil pipelines. An American official was quoted as saying, "We don't trust Turkey on this. They will keep the pipelines open to fill their own needs."

We speculated that the reason there was no news about us or any of the other hostages was that the world was not really interested. Osman had suggested that one reason Saddam Hussein had taken hostages was to shift the world's attention away from the occupation of Kuwait itself. But it didn't seem to be working that way.

There were reports on a Turkish radio station that thirty U.S. bombers had been flown to the Incirlik airbase in southern Turkey, and that large numbers of other U.S. military aircraft had been brought to the British base in Cyprus. It seemed that the Americans were preparing to attack Iraq. We were thinking that an American invasion might foment a popular revolution to overthrow the regime. Nonetheless, Saddam Hussein was showing no signs of being willing to give up Kuwait.

It was also reported that two U.S. naval groups were already in the Gulf but that others were still en route. Taner said, "That means we will be here for at least another week."

"Not necessarily," I said. "America has enough forces in the Gulf to wipe out Iraq right now. It doesn't have to wait for more to arrive."

At 8:20 pm, the BBC reported that groups of foreigners were beginning to evacuate Iraq through Jordan. That suggested to us that foreign nationals had been advised by their embassies to leave.

Husnu said it meant the embassies thought Iraq was going to be attacked, that bombs would soon be raining down.

I remembered what Osman had said that morning. "In this shed I feel like a chicken locked in a cage."

I said to everyone that we had to make ourselves even more prepared - we should plan how we would communicate among ourselves if the camp was bombed during an attack, and how we would implement an escape plan to avoid a panicked rush for the door. I asked Mehmet Cetinkoprulu and Ozer to work on this so that we could all agree on the final details.

We continued to theorize about why Saddam Hussein was allowing foreign nationals to leave Iraq. Taner suggested that Saddam seemed to want to act in accordance with international law. But others pointed out that Saddam was rarely concerned with abiding by international laws.

Margaret Thatcher and other figures on the Voice of America said that the economic embargo would not seriously affect Iraq for a long time. We were coming to the same conclusion as Thatcher - that there was no way to get Iraq out of Kuwait except through the use of force.

Just then, one of the guards blew a whistle, opened the door and ordered us out of the shed. At first, no-one moved. We did not know why we were being called and everyone seemed to fear the worst. Were we to be lined up in front of a firing squad and executed?

A number of the guards came in, gesturing with their weapons, yelling for us to get out. Seeing there was no choice, we reluctantly began to exit the shed. They started to line us up in rows of three in the courtyard and to count us. It turned out to be just another arbitrary counting of the hostages. After all of us had been jammed into the courtyard, we were ordered back into the shed.

Husnu gave us another review of the news. Taner beseeched us not to dwell on the worst implications, but we told him we had to consider every eventuality or be caught off guard. I thought myself that there was a strong possibility that Baghdad, and maybe the base where we were being held, would be bombed.

We also considered the possibility that if Iraq were attacked, Saddam Hussein would bomb these sheds and blame our deaths on the U.S. and whatever other countries were involved, saying to the world, "Look, you killed your own people."

It was certainly possible because, as everyone knew, Saddam Hussein was capable of anything; he was a cold-blooded killer. It made our skin crawl just to think what kind of nightmare we could face - the door locked, the guards fleeing and leaving us trapped like rats, soon to become barbecued rats.

At 9:30 pm, a guard opened the door and said something in Arabic. The only word we understood was "Chinese." It turned out he was calling for the Chinese to come out. Some of the prisoners congratulated the Chinese, assuming that they were going to be released. We figured that it was possible the Chinese were in fact being released, because holding them as hostages would not do Saddam Hussein much good.

It felt good because it looked as though at least one group was being released. But on the pessimistic side, there was more reason for Saddam to keep holding the other national groups.

Soon after, we were surprised when the guards called for the Turkish group to come out. We were taken into a hallway off the courtyard, where three Iraqi officers sat at a small table. They asked us for our addresses both in Turkey and in Kuwait. We were hesitant about giving them our addresses in Kuwait, fearing they might go to pillage and occupy our residences there. So, we gave them the address of the TJV guest house in the Salva region of Kuwait. That way we didn't have to worry about them going to our homes and looting our computers, software, checkbooks and other valuables.

The guards then started bringing the other national groups into the hall and it became very crowded. Slowly, they started calling out the other nations, as well as groups from the second large shed. It was the first time we had met any of those prisoners and we got to know yet more of the hundreds of people from all over the world who were trying to survive in the place.

Then there was another surprise. The guards brought a television into the courtyard and set it up on a table against one of the walls. It did not have an antenna, so they strung wires up over the roof. When they turned it on, the picture was fuzzy.

We watched a news program broadcast on Iraqi state television. It was all about Saddam from beginning to end. There was footage and news about him, delivered in a completely devotional tone, punctuated by a woman coming on the screen to sing songs of praise for him.

At one point, an announcer came on the screen and reported that Saddam had said that Kuwaitis were also Arabs, and that their lives and property would be protected by Iraq. As the announcer was reciting his lines, a photograph of Saddam, a headshot, would flash onto the screen.

In the meantime, I noticed that along the wall past the television, was an unmarked entrance to what turned out to be a small infirmary where they had put a few of the hostages who had become sick or were disabled. Amazingly, hidden in the back, I discovered a tiny shower. The drain was so completely clogged that by the time I had showered the filthy water was nearly up over my feet. Still, it was my first opportunity in five days, and I don't think I have ever appreciated a shower so much. I told some of the other engineers and they were able to shower as well. By the time they had finished, the water was nearly up to knee level.

More news from the radio. There was a report that Turkey had shut down the pipeline from Iraq and declared its full support for the economic embargo against Iraq. For his part, Saddam Hussein said he would retaliate if there was any attempt to forcibly remove Iraqi forces from Kuwait. Hearing these developments, I was sure that war against Iraq could happen at any time.

We agreed that three of us would stay outside the shed that night and take turns on watch until morning. We then appointed three people to keep watch on the inside. In this way, if anything happened we would know about it immediately, and we would have a chance to overpower the guards and get the door open if they fled during a bombing.

We also decided to approach the other national groups about cooperating in our emergency plan. I consulted with the Pakistani man named Hijaz and he thought it was a good idea. He said that each of the national groups had leaders and that I should talk with them. He said he would inform the leaders of the Pakistani, Indian and Philippine groups and have them come visit me.

Eventually, we brought together the largest groups in the shed - the Indians, who were close to three hundred, the

Pakistanis, who were about forty, nearly thirty from the Philippine group, and the Chinese, who were divided into two groups, one with about a hundred and twenty-five and the other with about twenty-five. The Chinese, younger and in very good physical shape, were very serious people.

I then went to the smaller shed to get the Europeans involved. But they became very nervous and were afraid of organizing or doing anything at all that might irritate the Iraqis. The reason was that they had been told by Iraqi officers that Saddam Hussein and Kuwaiti Emir Al-Sabah were going to travel to New York to meet with U.S. President Bush to resolve the crisis. Amazingly, they believed it.

Later, no-one could sleep. We believed that bombs could start dropping at any moment and were startled by any unexpected noise, even someone knocking on the door to go outside and use the toilet.

I managed to doze off for a while, but woke up around 1 am and saw that the guards had brought in some food. It consisted of the usual hard bread and some strange-colored liquid the guards called "meat juice." I decided to stay with just the bread and some water.

Wednesday, August 8th, 1990

When I woke up, people were going about the morning routine. The door was open so that everyone could get back and forth to the bathroom facilities in the courtyard.

Husnu checked the radio, as we were all curious about what had happened following the news last night that pointed to imminent war.

According to the Voice of America, the U.S. was poised to intervene militarily because of the ill treatment of Americans in Kuwait by the Iraqi occupation forces. With a possible invasion in mind, the U.S. was trying to bring together a coalition of Arab countries to cooperate in any military effort. It was also reported that more U.S. military units were arriving in Saudi Arabia and that a total of three aircraft carrier groups and fifty ships from the U.S. and other nations were now in the Gulf.

On the diplomatic front, there was constant communication between Bush, Thatcher and Egyptian leader Hosni Mubarak, and it was confirmed that Turkey had joined the embargo, with food and medicine being the only exceptions.

Pondering the morning's news, we all agreed that America had decided to attack, and had probably made its decision the day when Washington stated that it would defend Saudi Arabia.

President Bush was now trying to convince the American people that military action was needed, using the pretext of Iraq's ill treatment of Americans. At the same time, we thought, America wanted to gain the support of Arab countries, to avoid having sole responsibility, as it had in Vietnam.

We could not agree on the likely time of military intervention - tonight, in a few days? Ahmet Nakiboglu, Osman, Ozer and I were sitting on the floor, leaning back against the wall. Taner was standing in front of us with a look of fear in his eyes. He reminded me of a trembling skeleton. Most of our construction workers had gone back to sleep. Two of them were standing and listening.

Finally Ahmet said, "Nobody is going to bomb this camp or even Baghdad." I wished I could agree with him.

Ozer said that our worker Mehmet had scavenged a piece of metal that we could use to break open the fiberglass sheets in the ceiling. That way, he said, in an emergency we would be able to escape through the roof.

Osman, Mehmet Cetinkoprulu, Sedat and Ahmet Nakiboglu huddled together to go over the options for the escape plan. Taner tried to listen but seemed bewildered.

At about 8 am, we heard a jet plane fly overhead and another one a moment later. There was quiet for a while, but then more jets passed overhead. We were terrified by the thought of bombs dropping at any time.

We discussed stepping up cooperation between the national groups in our shed. The idea was to have two representatives from each nation to organize their own groups and to communicate with the other groups.

Taner interrupted. He said that Saddam Hussein was a maniac who was capable of anything. No one could know what he would do next. Taner wanted to know why Saddam had not told the world that he was holding all these people here. We told Taner we thought it was because Saddam was holding us as a last resort, that he would use us as bargaining chips when he had no other leverage. For the time being, we were his insurance.

More news came in over the radio. It was confirmed that Turkey had closed the oil pipeline from Iraq. It was also reported that twenty B-24 military aircraft had been mobilized at the Diyarbakir airbase in southeastern Turkey, and that thirty-nine Americans were being held in a hotel in Baghdad and were being described as "hostages."

Meanwhile, there was a report that Iraq was allowing nine Japanese tourists to leave through Jordan. We felt that might be a good sign, that maybe it meant that Mr. Tanaka, the leader of the Japanese group held along with the Europeans in the smaller shed, would be released too. If so, then he, like the rest of the group leaders, had a list of all the hostages and would notify everyone's embassy.

One of the reports concerned the economic ramifications of Iraq's occupation of Kuwait. For one thing, the Iraq-imposed government had devalued the Kuwaiti dinar by two-thirds, so that one Kuwaiti dinar was now equivalent to one Iraqi dinar. Saddam again had made a speech about how the rich Kuwaitis had been exploiting Iraq for so many years. And the Iraqi Ministry of Oil stated that the rise in oil prices was artificial, the result of speculation.

The BBC reported that London had ordered British citizens to leave Saudi Arabia immediately. We speculated that the way was being cleared for an invasion of Kuwait. Saddam continued to state that Iraqis would rather die than give up Kuwait.

Still, the reports said that there were now 30.000 U.S. troops in the Gulf, a relatively small number compared with the size of the Iraqi military. We thought maybe that was why the U.S. was bringing elements of its Atlantic fleet into the Gulf. These reports seemed to suggest there might still be some time before military intervention. The idea of spending more time in this place waiting for something to happen was discouraging to say the least.

I related to Hijaz the Pakistani and to Georgy, one of the Indian group, what we had been hearing on the radio. I told them about the huge U.S.-led military buildup in the Gulf and said that in the end we were likely to be bombed by either the Americans or Saddam Hussein. I told them to bring this to the attention of their groups, and said that because of the danger we needed to coordinate the efforts of the various groups, to defend ourselves and to escape if necessary.

I told them to pass along the information quietly, that we did not want to start a panic or arouse suspicion among the Iraqi guards. We also had to be careful in case any of the prisoners had become informers for the Iraqis. We could not afford to have the Iraqis suddenly increase the number of guards or lock us down any tighter. The idea was to go about preparing everyone in the shed, but in a very low-key way. I suggested that each group draw up an inventory of their members to see what role they could best play in a possible escape. Who had military training, who was the most physically fit, who had technical skills such as the ability to drive trucks or military vehicles?

I emphasized that the idea was to have a plan only for the event of an emergency - it was a question of self-defense and getting out alive if bombs began dropping or there were some other type of attack. The leaders of the groups should stay in communication in case something happened, and in particular to prevent people being crushed to death during a rush for the door.

Finally, I told them that once we were free, we wanted to file a human rights case against Saddam Hussein at The Hague or another international venue and that all the groups were welcome to join in the legal action. I told them we would be preparing a list of names and addresses of all those who wanted to participate.

I had the same conversation with the leaders of the two Chinese groups, a man named Suradet, who headed a group of about one hundred people, and a man called Son Pong, whose group had about twenty-five people.

Later, one of the leaders of the Indian group came to me and said that he did not want to provide names, even his own - that addresses would be sufficient. He said to communicate to him only through Georgy. I was wary of this man.

It was mid-morning and the door was opened for a bathroom break. There were dozens of people using cups and maybe a sliver of soap to try to clean themselves. The toilets were backing up and a pool of urine was spreading across the courtyard. The air was suffocating.

Looking around in disgust, Husnu said, "During the war between North and South in the United States, a hundred and fifty years ago, a general from the South was hung for running a prison camp like this one."

For some reason the guards were more abrasive today. They were yelling, shouting, pushing and slamming the door open and shut. At one point our construction workers almost got into a physical struggle with them during some kind of verbal confrontation. Our worker Mehmet, the one who knew some Arabic and was in with one of guards, managed to step in and calm things down.

After the first meal, one of the guards showed up with some tea. A long line immediately formed, with people pushing and shoving to get a place. In response, another guard barged in, striking randomly at people with a whip.

Around noon, after things had settled down, a group of Iraqi soldiers came and called for the Chinese and the Bangladeshis to line up. Names were called and recorded - just another random head count.

At the time I was out in the courtyard with the Europeans. The television on the table was announcing every ten minutes that a very crucial message from Saddam regarding the Arabs and the foreigners in Iraq would be broadcast at 6:30 pm. There was a rumor that a television would actually be brought into the shed. Earlier we had heard on the radio that President Bush was expected to make a speech around the same time. We were not expecting positive developments.

After I went back inside the shed soldiers came again and ordered everyone out. People were reluctant because it was the hottest part of the day. Finally, the soldiers, shouting and pushing, got everyone outside for yet another head count. I was near one of the faucets and tried to cool my head. But after just a few minutes the sun had already baked me dry.

Everyone was ordered back into the shed except for the Thai group. After a while, the Thais had not returned. Were they being counted again? Some in our group said maybe they were being released, while others speculated they were being moved to another shed. I joked that we had lost one of the teams for carrying our escape plan.

Ali R. Bozkurt

Husnu heard a report on the radio that Saddam Hussein had called on all Arabs to join him in a "holy war." He was asking Arabs to fight on his side in the name of Islam. This was probably to be Saddam's "crucial message" on Iraqi state television later on.

The theme of holy war had been used more frequently since the war between Iraq and Iran. Originally, a holy war would be called when a Muslim country was fighting against or had been attacked by a non-Muslim country. The idea was that all Muslim countries would join as one in the war and help the brother country for the sake of Islam. But the term holy war could have no meaning when one Muslim country, Iraq, had attacked another, Kuwait. Saddam's call for a holy war could not be taken seriously.

Osman pointed out that the Europeans had been taken prisoner right in front of a European ambassador, yet there still had been no mention of this on any of the news broadcasts we had heard. We surmised that the international community was trying to act as if the hostages mattered little to them, and in that way make Saddam think they were not much use as bargaining chips.

Our worker Ahmet again came to me to say that he could overpower all the guards in the courtyard by himself, that he was just waiting for a green light.

"How will you accomplish that?" I asked him.

He said he would take the first guard's gun and use it to disarm the other guards.

I repeated that he should not act on his own. I told him that to try it would be very dangerous, especially if he failed; realistically, it would take at least three people for it to work. I insisted to him that he wait until we had made a decision.

Meanwhile, a few of the engineers had managed to become friendly with some of the guards. That, plus the camp commander's order that I should be given what I asked for, made it possible for me, Mehmet Cetinkoprulu and Osman to sleep in the smaller shed where the Europeans and the Japanese were. We had decided that if there was a bombing attack during the night, this would be the best guarantee of ensuring that everyone got out of the larger shed.

It was quite crowded in the smaller shed and it took a while for the three of us to fit in. We ended up near the entrance, next to the Hungarians, including the young, overweight one with a beard, who was sleeping just as he was the last time I'd seen him. Next to him were the Hungarian boat captain and his crew. Also nearby were Mr. Tanaka and a Canadian named Patrick, who were both wearing beach hats, and a very young Malaysian named David, who was asleep. Both Mr. Tanaka and Patrick seemed to be in their fifties and in good physical shape. Patrick told us he was fifty-eight but that he was "an old man, young at heart."

Osman lay down in front of the door, while Mehmet Cetinkoprulu and I found space by the wall across from it. As we were getting settled, we noticed that the Thai group were being put back in the larger shed; they had not been released.

It was late afternoon. Patrick was discussing something with the Greeks. The Japanese, a Chinese and two other people were holding a conversation in a corner. A Greek and a Spaniard were playing chess using a piece of cardboard upon which they had drawn the chess squares. Osman and I were lying down observing everyone else. There was a shallow plastic tray with water and ice resting on a wooden box in the middle of the room. There were a few blankets on the floor. The air was stifling.

The only advantage of this smaller shed was that the door was not locked and we were able to go in and out of the courtyard at any time. Most importantly, we could quickly get the door to the larger shed open in the event of an emergency. And, as arranged earlier, Husnu had drawn a skeleton head that he would hang in the little window of that door if he heard on the radio that an attack on Iraq was underway and it was time to get the hell out.

Husnu continued monitoring the news and relaying it to us during bathroom breaks. As evening approached it was reported that Washington had said that the U.S. would not initiate a military operation until their forces deployed in the region were equal to those of Iraq. We found that hard to believe as the U.S. advantage would not be a question of troop size but of high-technology weaponry. We thought that Washington was trying to create some kind of diversion with its statement and that, in reality, there could be an attack at any moment.

The scenario we envisioned was that U.S.-led forces would invade from Saudi Arabia into the western Kuwaiti area of Al-Jahrah and across the border further west directly into Iraq, while simultaneously bombing Basra and Baghdad from the air. Israel, meanwhile, taking advantage of the situation, would target the chemical weapon and long-range missile installations it had identified in Iraq.

As always, there was the question of what would happen to the hostages in the event of an invasion. The Europeans were still optimistic, hoping to be released the next day. Someone in the shed, however, joked that if there was no release tomorrow, then we'd have to wait another three days because of the weekend.

Husnu came to report that President Bush had given his speech, outlining the deployment of U.S. air and ground forces in the region and noting that no U.S. president had ever ordered such a large military presence in the Gulf. He pointed out that Iraq, the second largest oil-producing country, with an army of one million, had declared that it would not invade Kuwait and had broken its commitment. It had then promised to leave Kuwait and broken that promise too. Bush said that the world was not fooled by Iraq showing over and again the same footage of a ship leaving Kuwait, and that Saddam Hussein had proven himself to be a liar. He then talked about all the diplomatic contacts being made by Secretary of State Baker: OPEC, Russia, Japan, Turkey, Great Britain and France all supported the U.S. position, and Turkish President Turgut Ozal was one of America's most dependable allies.

Another report said that Washington would not pull back U.S. troops unless Iraq withdrew completely from Kuwait and the old government was reinstated. It was also reported that had Britain offered to provide its own troops for the effort, but that Egypt and Morocco had said they would not.

On the economic front, OPEC announced that it would increase oil production to help keep oil prices stable.

Husnu said that he believed America would wait for a couple more days, organize its forces and then attack.

Taner suggested that America would not attack Iraq without the okay of Saudi Arabia. Therefore it would first try to get Iraq to leave Kuwait through economic pressure. But if there were an invasion, Turkey would be allied with the U.S. That would mean we would be in really hot water. Probably we would be shot.

Mehmet Cetinkoprulu assured Taner that we would not be executed. He said that if there were a war, the worst thing would be having to stay in this place for another two weeks, after which Iraq would be defeated.

At 6:30 pm, Saddam Hussein finally appeared on television to deliver his message. He declared that Kuwait was now part of Iraq, that Kuwait City was an important Iraqi port in the Gulf, and that he would fight to keep Kuwait until his last breath. Kuwait and Iraq were now united and because Kuwait was vulnerable Iraq would do everything to defend her.

Saddam's speech did not attract much of an audience among the hostages. There were only about twenty viewing the screen in the courtyard, along with seven or eight Iraqi soldiers.

So both Bush and Saddam had made their statements and it did not seem that there would be any peaceful resolution to the crisis. If anything, events seemed to be accelerating toward armed confrontation.

I thought to myself how we were completely caught up in something that didn't concern us and how we had absolutely no say in the matter. It was as if we were in an automobile, speeding toward a certain crash, and although we could clearly see it coming, the brakes were out, the edge of the cliff was fast approaching and, because we were tied up in the back seat, no-one could reach the steering wheel.

At about 9:30 pm, the guards brought the usual hard bread and "meat juice." But then they came with the surprise of the night - some fruit. Mr. Tanaka had requested it from one of the guards the night before and had offered him some money, which the guard declined. But he said that he would try and here he was with a bit of watermelon and a few bunches of grapes. There were twenty-three of us in the small shed, so, after washing the grapes as best we could, we divided them up evenly, about four grapes per person. It was the first real food we had been given in nearly a week and there is nothing like being starved to make one appreciate the value of fresh food, especially fruit. We decided to save the watermelon for the following day - having two kinds of fruit in one day was too much of a luxury.

Meanwhile, a news program was on the television out in the courtyard. A tall Jordanian prisoner, a nurse, translated from the Arabic for us. Iraq claimed that Israel was painting the American flag on its airplanes. Therefore, if the U.S. attacked Iraq, Iraq said it would launch a missile with a chemical weapon warhead against Israel. Iraq also said that it had made a non-aggression pact with Saudi Arabia but that the Saudis had broken it by allowing foreigners to enter into the holy areas. Therefore, Iraq was now free to attack Saudi Arabia. Finally, Iraq reaffirmed that it would never give up Kuwait.

Saddam Hussein then came back on the screen and started making another speech. He was sitting on a high platform wearing a military uniform, while behind was a portrait of him dressed in a suit jacket. On either side of him were two guards who seemed to be aiming their guns at the members of the executive council listening to his speech. Loud applause by the council members followed his every sentence, but would end abruptly with a wave of Saddam's hand. One of the Greek hostages sitting next to me said that it was admirable how well the council behaved and said that it must be quite interesting to work with a council whose members were so supportive.

A number of other prisoners also seemed to admire Saddam's method of rule, the way one gesture was enough to turn the applause on and off, the way nobody would criticize him.

But this was rule through fear. He terrorized everyone beneath him so that people had to act as if everything he did or said was divine. Those who envied such a system were being hypocritical. It is not about a style of governing, but a deep-seated problem often found in poorer countries where citizens could not fully develop as people. If an individual was even a little successful, then others would kiss his ass, seeking favors. That would lead the successful one to believe that he was superior and, in extreme cases, that he had divine powers. In such an atmosphere, people would actually seek out and embrace dictators to rule over them. I thought that if Saddam were deposed, he would probably be followed by another dictator who also would go mad, intoxicated by own sense of being a god.

Meanwhile, I believed that the radio reports indicated that we were clearly hostages and in a very precarious position with the threat of war mounting. Some type of attack on Baghdad seemed inevitable, which meant that we would either die in a massive bombing or escape into a city in total chaos. The only positive thing we could glean from today's reports was that the day of reckoning might be delayed, that we might be "guests" here a while longer before all hell broke loose. We decided that for now it was best to remain vigilant, to keep up our endurance and stay prepared for anything.

Midnight was approaching. Husnu, Mehmet Cetinkoprulu and I were out in the courtyard talking. We saw forty or fifty people coming into the prison compound carrying suitcases. They seemed relaxed and well prepared. At first we thought that they might even be Iraqi soldiers coming here to spend the night. Later, we found out that they were actually Kuwaiti citizens who had been taken from their homes. Apparently they had been given enough time to pack some belongings. So now the Iraqis were abducting Kuwaitis from their homes and bringing them all the way to Baghdad.

It seemed to us that the Iraqis had now developed some kind of systematic process for internment, that the procedures for taking and holding prisoners had become very organized, even disciplined. It suggested to us that Iraq was in the hostage business for the long term and that any light we had been able to see at the end of the tunnel had just gone out. That night was probably our most fitful and distressed so far.

Thursday, August 9th, 1990

Osman, Mehmet Cetinkoprulu and I woke up with the Europeans. We called them the EEC group because they represented so many member countries of the European Economic Community. In the larger shed I had been sleeping on some cardboard. But here we had to lie down on bare cement. Osman and Mehmet Cetinkoprulu kidded me that I was finally going to get in shape. They said that I looked sharp that morning, that my paunch was beginning to disappear.

The sun was again climbing into a bright, cloudless sky and the temperature was already rising rapidly. The rest of our group were out in the courtyard for the first morning break. They told us that earlier that morning Sedat had got the approval of the guards to organize everyone to clean the large shed.

With all seven hundred or so prisoners working at the task and Sedat and others moving the garbage out, Sedat had been able to do some reconnaissance. He said that the perimeter of the compound was only two hundred meters away, and that on the other side of the wall was a busy city street with civilian traffic flowing by. We had not known about this when we had devised an escape route using the long road that led out to the front entrance. With this new information, we decided to draw a new map of the compound and revise our plan.

The courtyard was extremely crowded and I was told that people were using other toilets down through a passageway. These toilets were for the hundreds of people in the other large shed. There were about twenty stalls but only two were functional as far as I could tell. The layers of scum and sewage from the overflowing tanks were even more putrid than in the courtyard. People were gagging.

I went to the end of the line to wait my turn. In front of me was an Indian man, about fifty years old, with a beard and ponytail. He told me that back in Kuwait, when he had heard the country was being invaded, he had told his son to stay inside their home while he went out to see what was happening. Within moments soldiers had arrested him on the street and taken him away. He felt sure that his son was still in Kuwait but was very worried about him.

I asked him if he knew why there were so many Indians in this camp - four hundred and five of them by their own count. He said he didn't, but that he believed the Indians were being held by Iraq for the same reason as everyone else - to be used as bargaining chips. We agreed that with hostages from so many countries we were like a United Nations behind bars.

In spite of everything, he was very upbeat. While waiting in line, he performed some simple magic tricks and told riddles and jokes that people enjoyed. It got some of the most dejected prisoners to smile. I saw that in the worst of circumstances, even the smallest things could help give people a lift. The Indian man's spirit and refusal to give into the anxiety and fear that we were all living acted like a painkiller for others. Having an attitude like his can be very useful in life.

I returned to go to the small shed and came across Taner, who was in the courtyard during a break. He said that his blood pressure was going down because his supply of salt tablets had run out two days ago. He had asked the Pakistani doctor if he could have some but had not received any. He said that the low blood pressure could put him in shock at any moment.

Taner indeed looked terrible, his skin was pale and he was very weak. So I went immediately to the doctor and explained the situation to him. He told me that he had requested salt tablets as well as other medications but that so far the Iraqis had provided nothing. He told me that he was aware of Taner's condition but that there was little he could do: he wasn't able to obtain any natural salt even.

Later, I noticed that the Iraqi doctor had entered the courtyard and that he and the Pakistani physician were talking. The Iraqi doctor said he had given a list of medications to his superiors but had yet to receive a response. He was a young, mild-mannered man who spoke English well.

Angrily, I told him, "You don't need a list just to get a handful of salt. You couldn't even ask your wife to put a spoonful of salt in a small paper to bring here? Where is your sense of responsibility as a physician? And what's more, even animals could not survive in this camp under these conditions, let alone human beings."

Suddenly, I felt fingers poking me in the back and hands pulling me away by my arms and shoulders. It was some our engineers and a few of the Europeans; they had overheard me and were trying to calm me. But I kept on, telling the doctor about those who were hanged in America a hundred and fifty years ago because they had allowed inhuman conditions in the prison camps during the war between the North and South. I said to him that he might be in control at the moment, but someday he could find himself trying to explain his complicity in war crimes to an international court.

I said to him, "Shooting people is not the only way of killing them. A contagious disease could easily break out and kill more than half of the people here in one day. As a doctor, you should know this better than anybody else here. The orders given to you by your superiors do not release you from your duty as a physician."

I also told him that his superiors would most likely lie if they were ever brought to trial and claim that they were not even informed about the camp conditions. In that case, the full responsibility would fall on him, the camp doctor.

At that moment Mehmet Dural Baran came over and I asked the doctor if the Iraqi Minister of Social Affairs had been informed that the Minister and Mehmet were cousins. The doctor said he had informed the officers in charge of the camp. I became angry again, shouting that he should have made sure that the Minister himself was informed, as it could have meant our release, or at least Mehmet's.

The doctor became defensive, saying that the Iraqi soldiers had to live in this camp under the same conditions. I replied that he could not be so ignorant or innocent as to think that the position of Iraqi soldiers and civilians could be compared. I said that the people here had been abducted from their hotels and that some even had diplomatic passports. I told him I would be eager to be the first witness to testify at his trial. And if I was no longer alive, then someone else who survived this hell would step up to tell the court about the conditions here. He would be condemned in the eyes of the world.

The doctor had become anxious; he was on the verge of panic, it seemed. He stared at me for a moment with frightened, bewildered eyes. Then he said, "No more," and quickly walked away. By that time, I was pretty shaken myself and it took a while before I was able to simmer down.

Husnu told us he had heard on the radio that the Iraqis had released a British and a German hostage and that they had been freed at the border with Jordan. Although there were few details of the release, the European prisoners became very excited when I told them. Meanwhile, we ate the watermelon left over from the day before. Mr. Tanaka spent what seemed like half an hour using sign language to get one of the guards to loan him a small knife to cut it into pieces.

I realized that the Europeans might have a better chance of being released than the rest of us. So I gathered our entire group in the courtyard and made sure that at least one person from each European country, as well as Mr. Tanaka, had a complete list of names of our group, with telephone numbers and home addresses. We asked them to the give list of our people to the Turkish embassy if they were released.

Meanwhile, Osman wrote a letter from us to the embassy. to be taken along with the list:

"Your Excellency, we are members of a Turkish construction company, abducted from Kuwait and now being held prisoner in Baghdad. We have heard no mention of ourselves on the radio. We have heard that Germans and British who were also abducted have been released. We hope that you will expend every effort to secure our freedom and we believe that our government has the power to do it. Forty-three Turkish people are struggling to survive here amid shit and urine under extremely difficult conditions. Our only strength and support is God. With all due respect..."

Meanwhile, we had just about completed the compilation of all the names and personal data for each nationality - part of the overall planning I was coordinating with the other national group leaders in the large shed. At one point I met in the courtyard with Son Pong, leader of one of the Chinese groups. As we exchanged greetings and shook hands, I felt him release

118

a folded paper into my palm. I casually placed it in my pocket without the guards noticing. As I expected, I found out later that it was the pages from my notebook that I had given to him to record the names and data for the members of his group. This surreptitious passing of messages was like something we had seen in the movies.

Our worker Mehmet got into a dispute with one of the guards. Ever since our workers had run out of cigarettes, it had been difficult to keep them calm. I told them that we were doing everything possible under the circumstances and that they should try to get along with everyone, including the guards. I explained that disruptive actions could cause disrespect for our group and damage our authority. I suggested that if there were any further outbursts, they would have to be disciplined.

Our worker Ahmet was still determined to try to overwhelm the guards and take control of the camp. We explained to him that we were inside a military police base, with probably thousands of soldiers around us, and that the risks were far too great. He remained insistent.

One of the more amusing developments of the day was the attempt by the Europeans to write a letter to the base commander. One had actually been written the previous day and given to one of the guards to give to the commander. This had not worked when I had tried it, so I doubted there would be any response this time. Some had their hopes up, however, because one of the officers had said he would see to it that the commander received their letter.

But then an argument broke out about the letter between the two groups in the smaller shed: the Sheraton Group that included Mr. Tanaka, and the all-European group. The latter was upset because apparently Mr. Tanaka had written the first letter without telling them. One of them said to him, "We were going to write the letter together. Why did you write it without us?"

Mr. Tanaka said that they could write another letter themselves if they wanted. But the Europeans argued that since they were all stuck in this terrible situation they should maintain unity and act together. It seemed that the conditions of our confinement were starting to get to everyone.

An Australian from the Sheraton group held up his hands in despair. "Why did they take us from that hotel? There were people from Qatar, Egypt and Jordan there. They called us from our rooms and brought us here. We thought that the Iraqis were gathering only Europeans."

A Japanese man and a Hungarian started arguing about the letters, while the Australian was going on about something else. Osman and I were just sitting there trying to follow along. I tried to explain that any letter they wrote would probably never reach the commander and suggested that they stop arguing. They ignored me and the bickering continued on for some time.

Around mid-morning I went to the large shed. Inside it looked much better following the cleaning effort headed by Sedat. Because it was our group that had organized the cleaning and I was the one who had confronted the Iraqi doctor, many of the prisoners had come to see us in a leadership role. And since I had coordinated the exchange of lists and personal data with the other national groups, there was also the perception that we were the ones who would lead an escape attempt.

It was therefore no surprise when hostages from other groups increasingly came to us to complain about the conditions in the compound in the hope that we might be able to do something, that maybe some sort of protest could be organized.

In fact, the abysmal conditions seemed to be getting worse. The bathroom facilities continued to deteriorate and threatened to break down completely; the swarms of flies were becoming thicker and the food remained barely edible.

When the food arrived in the courtyard, representatives from each national group would line up at the metal door with food trays in hand, pushing and elbowing one another. The guards would start calling out names and nationalities: "Turgut, Turkey. Ho Mishi, China," and so on. Whenever a name was called, someone would burst through the door.

The food, which continued to be an awful tasting, soup-like substance, came in twenty-gallon buckets. The guards would scoop out a portion with a pot and give it to each representative, some of whom brought scarves or other pieces of clothing to carry the bread. Otherwise, the bread would be dumped into the pot. It was really something - watching people trying to take the bread out of the soup. It seemed like they were fishing. In the process, they were spilling the stuff all down the sides of the pot.

If someone needed to get out into the courtyard in between the breaks, to use the toilets or to get water, then he would have to bang on the door for five minutes, ten minutes, or until whenever a guard came to open it. Sometimes the guards would shout at the person wanting to get out, maybe push them around and slam the door back in their face. It usually depended on the mood of the guards whether someone could get out. But many of the prisoners were becoming less fearful and more demanding. Or maybe it was just that under the circumstances they were becoming more desperate.

Head counts would be taken at least two or three times a day, and sometimes more often. It was done country by country, group by group. The place was becoming like a

United Nations circus, even as the rest of the world remained unaware of what we were going through.

The mood became calmer as the afternoon faded. But always there was the underlying sadness and concern because of our isolation, that gnawing emptiness that never went away as we thought of our families, not knowing how they were doing, and they not knowing whether we were dead or alive.

As evening approached, Husnu monitored the news broadcasts. Apparently, little had changed. The BBC commented that the U.S. was still not fully prepared to launch an attack but other reports suggested an invasion was close. As always we began an intense discussion. One view was that America could not attack before it had destroyed the chemical weapon installations in Iraq. Another was that not enough troops had been deployed in the region and that it might take another three to four days before they were ready. Taner replied to this in his usual dreary way: "Every time we hear news from some place, it costs us two more days in prison."

The BBC broadcast an interview with a former Iraqi general who had fled the country. He said there could be nothing in the world worse than the Saddam Hussein regime; even Hitler was not as bad. "We call him the Butcher of Baghdad." He said that Saddam had a pervasive intelligence network and that anyone exhibiting the slightest sign of opposition to his rule was killed immediately. That is why people tried to escape the country rather than challenge him.

Meanwhile, we received the names of forty-three Turks who were being held in the other large shed. They were drivers and laborers who had been abducted by Iraqi forces in Kuwait and brought here separately from us. We added their names to the list of our group that we had given to the leaders of the other national groups. The Europeans reiterated their promise to take the list to the Turkish authorities. Mr. Tanaka said, "I guarantee you that the first thing I will do when I get out of this place is to take this list to your embassy."

More news came in over the radio. Egyptian President Mubarak had called for an Arab summit and invited ten countries, as well as Palestinian leaders and the Al-Sabah family. He said it was Iraq's last chance to prevent foreign military intervention.

The guard who had brought the fruit the other day brought a few biscuits. Each one was divided up between about ten people. It was a small treat during another day of searing heat, dripping sweat, misery and fear.

I went over to see our group in the large shed as the evening meal was brought in. It was far less than usual, just a meager bowl of rice and a few pieces of bread and it was in such a rotten state that most of us could not eat it. Some of us wondered if the Iraqis were trying to make us even weaker from hunger so that we would be easier to control.

Suddenly the steel door banged open and a group of five Iraqi soldiers came in. One of the officers had clusters of three stars on his epaulets, and we wondered whether he was a general. Accompanying him was the Iraqi doctor I had rebuked that morning. There was a sudden stir among the hostages but it subsided quickly, probably our of fear. Still, hunger overcame fear for some of the hostages as they approached the senior officer, complaining about the meager portions of food.

The Iraqi officers ignored the complaints and turned to leave. One of them looked toward our group, pointed to me and said, "Come."

Some in my group had criticized me for reprimanding the doctor, saying that I had acted as if he was my hostage and not the reverse. They also reminded me about the journalist working for the British press who had been hung by the Iraqi regime for being a spy, despite formal protests from London. Despite pressure from all over the world, Saddam Hussein had gone ahead and killed the man, Margaret Thatcher had said.

Osman said to me, "Saddam is crazy. One cannot deal with this regime in a civilized manner." He warned me to be very careful. "You have to watch yourself when you're speaking to these people. It might cost you your life and put the rest of us in jeopardy as well."

I could see that everyone else looked nervous and scared. I barely had time to grab my shoes before being led away.

When I got outside, the Hungarian with the wife was telling the officers how he had been seized from his ship with her left behind in a hotel. "What will happen to her?" he asked. The officer with the three stars said with a smirk, "Don't worry; we will take care of her."

When they saw me coming, the officers turned in my direction. The one with the stars said he was the base commander and asked, "So, what is your complaint?"

"Holding all these people here under these conditions is a form of murder," I replied.

The commander said, "We are protecting your lives."

"No," I said. "You are not protecting our lives; you are killing us. You are murderers, all of you are killers. Go and look at those toilets clogged with waste and spilling urine everywhere. For you to use the word 'protect' cannot even be considered a joke. You know full well that at least half the people here will die in this filth, either of hunger or of disease. And for that you will certainly be judged one day in a court of law. If any of us get out alive to testify, I believe that you will be hung for crimes against humanity."

At that moment, the Iraqi doctor turned to me and said, "You see, I am not guilty. I have transferred your complaint to my commander."

I said, "Yes, we have no case against you any longer. You did what we asked."

The Commander turned and stormed out of the courtyard with the other officers.

I went back inside the shed and was surrounded by my colleagues and members of some of the other groups. All were eager to hear what had happened, but I could not really tell them what I had said to the commander. Trying to ease their anxiety, I said, "Don't worry. Hopefully, everything will be fine in a day or two and we will be out of this place."

Things settled down after a while and people returned to their routines. The buzz of so many conversations in such a small, confined space made it sound as if we were inside a stadium. The Chinese were among the youngest of the hostages. One of the Chinese groups had actually formed a simulated orchestra, with individuals using their voices to mimic the sounds of the different instruments. This joyful exercise seemed to give everyone a lift.

The radio reported two serious developments. The first was that the U.S. military was now withholding information regarding its deployments and maneuvers in the Gulf. The other was that Iraq had reversed its decision to permit foreigners to leave. It seemed that the winds of war were blowing harder again.

The BBC was constantly trying to determine American intentions and at this point the indications were that

Washington was grappling with a number of issues in preparation for liberating Kuwait from Iraq. One was the question of chemical weapons - could the U.S. send forces into Kuwait without first neutralizing them, taking them out by aerial bombing or some other means? How long might that take? When would the U.S. military have what it considered a sufficient invasion force ready in Saudi Arabia.

For us, the main question was how Iraq would react in the event of an attack? Specifically, when and how would Iraq utilize its hostages? It was increasingly frustrating to hear nothing about us on the radio. There were seven hundred of us in our shed alone, hundreds more jammed into other sheds, and more being dragged in every day. Yet listening to the news broadcasts, it was as if we did not exist. How could this be?

Husnu theorized that the U.S. was blocking any mention of the hostages in the media. He suggested that the Americans were waiting until they were ready to attack; then they would use us to sway public opinion in favor of military intervention. "And it will work," he said.

Mehmet Cetinkoprulu said, "I don't believe that America would be so selfish and callous as to manipulate the hostages in that way."

Ozer said, only half facetiously, "We don't really know whose prisoners we are. Maybe we are actually the prisoners of the oil companies, who certainly have an interest in this conflict. Or maybe we are the prisoners of the weapons manufacturers, who also will profit from military intervention."

At that point the guards opened the metal door and people poured out into the courtyard for a break. Our worker Ahmet, who had been sleeping outside, told us a story. He said that one of the hostages, a young Palestinian man, had been moved into the infirmary, suffering from some kind of kidney problem. He had had to be taken to a hospital and Ahmet had been commandeered to help wrap him in a blanket and carry him out.

Ahmet had used the opportunity to look around. He said that he saw two guards stationed at the door leading out of the courtyard and two more at the next gate. He said that behind the small shed where the Europeans were, he had seen an area covered by barbed wire that led to some iron bars about ten meters away. Through those bars were two long ladders leaning against a wall. He believed that if we could get hold of one of those ladders and pull it through the bars, we could use it to get onto the roof of the small shed. From the roof we could get up and over the adjacent wall. On top of the wall was barbed wire, and broken glass was embedded in the concrete. Ahmet believed we could use the food trays stacked in the courtyard to protect out feet from the glass and blankets to cover the barbed wire. Once we were past the inner wall, we could use the ladder to get over the last barrier at the perimeter of the camp only a few hundred meters away and out into the streets of the city.

Using the information provided by Ahmet, we revised our map of the camp. We also decided that if we did escape it would not to be wise to go directly to the Turkish embassy, as the Iraqis would probably block the roads leading there once they discovered we were gone.

Mehmet Cetinkoprulu suggested that we should go to the offices of Kutlutas, the Turkish construction company for which he had once worked as a project manager. He knew the location of the building and most of the staff and said we could hide out there, at least for a few days.

Another option was proposed by Mehmet, the driver of our long-gone minibus. He suggested that we go to the Baghdad bus station. During previous driving jobs he had traveled to the station and he knew his way around it. He said there were always thousands of people going in and out and no-one would notice or bother us. Once there, we could telephone the Turkish embassy and have them send diplomatic vehicles for us. He also said that he knew where to contact Turkish truckers in Baghdad, who might be able to smuggle us all the way out of the country.

Someone jokingly suggested that we put on Iraqi military uniforms, go to the embassy, disarm the Iraqi guards and go on in. The only thing crazier than that scenario was that Saddam Hussein, a madman respecting no laws whatsoever, might then bomb our embassy.

As we talked, the guards brought the television back into the courtyard and again put it on the table by the wall. They turned it on and, although the reception was poor, we could still see demonstrations in support of Saddam - people dancing and singing his praises. If you looked closely, however, you could see that there were only a few hundred people, even though the cameras tried to make it look like thousands.

Next came a news program and the announcer said that economic and trade agreements between the previous Kuwaiti government and foreign companies would be respected by the new Iraqi regime. Upon hearing that we howled with laughter. TJV was the largest foreign company operating in Kuwait and its chairman, all its project managers and dozens of its workers were locked up in a Baghdad hellhole.

We had barely stopped laughing when the guards told the Europeans to assemble in the courtyard. It looked as though they might be preparing to release them and the Europeans were excited. But it turned out to be just another arbitrary head count. To temper their disappointment, the Europeans organized a maintenance program for the small shed, with everyone given an assignment. Someone would sweep the floor, someone else would organize the blankets, and so on. A handwritten schedule was put up on the wall and my name ended up at the top of the list for duty. I joked that if they were released I would have done all the work.

When the evening meal was brought in, we were surprised to find that there was meat in the soup and that it did not taste too bad. We wondered if all the complaining and noise we had been making was actually having an effect.

I ate in the courtyard with the Europeans. There were three trays and about ten of us huddled around each one. The trays were small and, although the food was edible today, there was not much of it. So, there we were, an array of top-management people from many different nations, naked from the waist up, pants in tatters, down on our knees, with no forks or spoons, using our fingers to get at what little food there was.

After eating, I noticed that the eyes of one of our workers, Metin, had become very red and irritated, so I showed the Pakistani doctor. He examined Metin and managed to find some eye drops. As he was a hostage, too, I felt a degree of trust with him. I explained to him that because of the possibility of attack, we needed our worker Mehmet to sleep out in the courtyard along with Ahmet. The doctor cleverly told the guards that Mehmet was suffering from diarrhea and needed unlimited access to the toilets, and the guard said Mehmet could sleep outside the shed.

Osman, Mehmet Cetinkoprulu, Ozer and I then worked on the organization of our teams, each one to be headed by an engineer. We decided that each team should also have at least one person skilled in driving various types of vehicles, one who spoke English, and one who spoke at least some Arabic.

I suggested that we consider not only ways of escaping from the camp, but also ways of overwhelming the guards on a bus or a truck in the event of our being transferred to another prison, or to a strategic site to be used as human shields. I said that all contingencies should be discussed and all final plans agreed by consensus.

I returned to the small shed to take notes of our discussions and prepare a list of our teams. As it was getting late, one of the Europeans turned off the dim bulb that barely made a dent in the darkness. I was able to keep writing by the thin band of light that came through the door from the courtyard.

It seemed that nearly everyone had fallen asleep when a guard abruptly showed up and began barking, "Spain, Hungary, Japan, Finland..." They all jumped for joy, as it seemed they were being released. Each one promised me that he would go to the Turkish embassy with the names of our group.

Patrick the Canadian and David from Sri Lanka had not been called and remained with me, Osman and Mehmet Cetinkoprulu. It was now 11 pm. The five of us straightened the place up, with the others now gone. I asked the guards if the other engineers could join us in this shed. One of them said it would be okay and a short while later they were brought in.

We explained to the rest of our group that the Europeans and Mr. Tanaka were apparently being released. Then we went over the list of teams we had prepared. I said that I would be leader of the first team and named the others who would be in it. Taner seemed greatly relieved when I said he would be part of my team. I felt it was best to have him with me, because he seemed calmer in my presence and I was concerned he might act precipitously in an emergency.

The other team leaders included Osman, Mehmet Cetinkoprulu and Ozer. I thought that Ozer's team was the strongest. It included Ibrahim Mender, along with Mehmet and some of the other Arabic-speaking workers, as well as workers with good driving skills. This team also had people who were the toughest among us physically. So we decided that it would be the fighter or point team - the one that would spearhead whatever escape operation we initiated if there were an attack or an emergency.

Patrick and David seemed bewildered by our level of organization and planning. But their jaws really dropped when I suggested that if we were not released by Saturday, August 11th, then we should carry out our plan for escape.

Osman said that Saturday was the first day of the week after the weekend: there would be a lot of paperwork to be done if we were to be released. So we should give it at least another day. Everyone agreed to push back the deadline until Sunday. By then it was nearly midnight and we decided to go to sleep.

Not long afterward, a guard came into the shed and shouted "Turkiya, Turkiya, Turkiya!" We all jumped up, nervous and alarmed. We were even more apprehensive when they told us to take our belongings, because we did not believe we were being released. So, what was happening? Were we being transferred to some other prison? Some secret place to be executed? As we gathered our things, we looked at each other with fear in our eyes. The situation had never been so tense.

The entire Turkish group was lined up in the courtyard in rows of five. We were then led out through the passageway, ankle deep in urine and scum, and through the metal doors into the central square where we had first arrived. We saw that other groups, thirty and forty and fifty people, were lined up and seated on the ground. We were counted one by one, then ordered to sit in rows next to a group of Iranians.

As we sat and waited, an Iraqi soldier who spoke some Turkish came over and said not to worry, that we would be released soon. Comforting words, but we had heard them before. We remained skeptical. He also said that we would be taken to Turkey on a Turkish Airlines flight. We were skeptical because we knew this tactic of giving false hope. After a while, we were ordered to stand and then to march toward some military trucks parked by the side of the square. I thought maybe we were going to be put into them, but we kept on walking, back through the metal doors and right into the prison courtyard yet again.

We were met by the guards and a young heavyset man who turned out to be the Jordanian of Palestinian descent whom Ahmet had helped carry out in the blanket when he became ill. He spoke English and seemed eager to act as a translator for the Arabic speaking guards. Then, when our workers started to move toward the smaller shed, hoping to join me and the engineers now that the Europeans were gone, the Palestinian wanted to stop them. He tried to convinced the guards that he, the Pakistani doctor and a few others should be in the smaller shed instead of us. When we tried to argue against that, we were sure he was not correctly translating our words to the guards, that he was telling them something about our group being willing to go to some different building.

Finally, I grabbed his wrist and told him we did not need him for a translator. He started yelling at me to let go and the guards stepped in between us. When all of us - engineers and workers - began walking to the small shed, the guards didn't stop us. We settled in as best we could, since all the blankets were now gone. Some of our workers said they had heard that the Palestinian was a spy for the Iraqis.

It was 2:30 am. We tried to sleep but the stress of the last few hours kept us awake. We could not help wondering whether we should move up our deadline and try to escape as soon as possible, or continue to wait. We still might be released, but then again they could transfer us to some worse place from which it would be impossible to escape.

When I woke up, the Morning Prayer was being called, so it must have been around 4:30 am. One of the guards was sleeping outside on a table. His name was Adil. He had been wounded in the war with Iran and was constantly showing off his scars and bragging about his exploits as a soldier.

Adil was the worst natured of the guards. Whenever he opened the door to the large shed, he would scream and yell at the prisoners and sometimes shove them around. Maybe he wasn't such a bad person - maybe these circumstances accentuated the worst of his personality. But sometimes he would behave like a child. Once when I was staying with the Europeans, he had come into the shed and placed match sticks on the ground in the shape of an airplane. He challenged us to change the direction in which the airplane was pointing by moving only three match sticks. He was very pleased when no one could figure it out and very arrogantly showed us how it was done.

It was strange having to deal with this adult child who was desperate for attention and at the same time our jailer. At one point, Mr. Tanaka had showed Adil a parlor trick he was not familiar with. Adil was stumped and when Mr. Tanaka refused to reveal the solution, Adil walked off in a huff. "Maybe that will keep him busy for a few days," Mr. Tanaka said.

Now, Adil was sleeping on the table next to our shed. When I passed by him on the way to the toilets I saw a second guard snoozing on another table. There were no other guards in sight. When I came back the second guard roused himself and asked if there were any others using the toilets. I said to him - half in English, half in Arabic - that there were, and he dozed off again. I then saw Sedat coming from the toilets. He said he had noticed the same thing - that at that hour, with the guards unable to stay awake, we could have walked right out of the courtyard.

Patrick the Canadian joined us. As he washed his hands at one of the leaky faucets, Sedat and I let him in on our plans for escape. He said trying to escape now was "dangerous and unnecessary." He said, "I think they will keep you here a while longer and then release you."

I still believed that we needed to prepare for every contingency and decided that when all the engineers were awake we would meet to go over final details and decide exactly how and when to proceed. This was a decision that would have to be made by consensus.

Back inside the shed I found that Taner was awake and in a very agitated state. He was shuffling through his belongings and stuffing some of them into a small bag. When I asked what he was doing, he said in a panicky voice, "They will take us to the southern front by train. I am taking only essential things like underwear. I will throw away the rest." He was in a terrible state, repeating himself and saying over and over, "They will take us to the front."

I tried to find a way to calm Taner down. He was in such bad shape that he might do more damage to himself than Saddam Hussein could. I told him that we needed to stay strong and to be prepared, and for that we should be rested. I told him that we had to trust in God, to put ourselves in the hands of God and to try to get some sleep.

Finally, he lay down near my feet, perpendicular to me. Mehmet Cetinkoprulu was sleeping on my right, while Ibrahim was next to him. Mehmet Dural Baran was next to Ibrahim, and next to them were Patrick and David. Our other engineers and workers were scattered throughout the room. Just before falling asleep, I saw that Taner was sitting up again fiddling with his stuff.

Friday, August 10th, 1990

It was 8:30 am when I awoke. For some reason, everyone in our group seemed to be in a better mood, maybe because we were all together again. People were laughing at the smallest things. Even Taner seemed to have gotten himself together and was making quips that had people laughing. Somebody remarked on how crazy it was the way we were taken out and counted at all hours and Taner said, "Most people count sheep if they can't go to sleep. When the commander of this place can't sleep, he counts prisoners."

After we had attempted to eat the usual meal of bread and sloppy lentil mush, one of the guards came and ordered us to get out of the shed and take all our belongings and blankets with us.

Out in the courtyard we sat in the shadow of the shed and watched as the guard carried an old metal table, a broken bench and some chairs into the small shed.

A little while later about a half dozen officers arrived. They wore blue hats and had blue epaulets, some with two stars. The officer who appeared to be in charge had an insignia of a sword on his uniform. One of the guards said he was a general.

As we watched, Patrick and David knelt down with us in the shade. Prisoners were being called from the large shed and sent into the small one. We assumed it was for interrogation. The food for those in the large shed remained out in the courtyard, dozens of trays of the soupy mush stacked zigzag by the door, flies buzzing all around. The weather was sunny and clear. And while it was hot, for a change there was a breeze and the air was not stifling. It almost felt relaxing.

We expected that we would also be interrogated by these officers who seemed to act like some type of war council. There was a sense of anticipation and anxiety, like waiting to be called for an exam.

We tried to imagine what it would be like to be in front of this council. Some of us remembered scenes from war movies in which death sentences were arbitrarily handed down in a matter of minutes as prisoners were brought in and out as if on an assembly line. Taner was sitting next to me trying to get straight in his mind what he would say. Ahmet Nakiboglu was trying to calm his nervous tics. Ibrahim seemed eerily quiet.

Another group of prisoners had been lined up in the courtyard to our left. One by one, they were called into the shed for two or three minutes at a time.

Finally, one of the officers approached us, asked if we spoke English and started calling us in. Osman went first, followed by me. I told the officers that we were a Turkish group from the TJV construction firm, and that all our top management and a number of our workers were here. Then I explained what we had been working on in Kuwait. I said, "Just when we had completed the construction site, you came and took us away."

They seemed to think that was funny.

I said, "President Saddam Hussein declared on television last night that all economic agreements undertaken by the Kuwaiti government would be honored by Iraq."

They chuckled again and nodded their heads.

"So, if that is true," I continued, "you should let us go so we can return to work at our construction site. Otherwise, the President will see that you are contradicting him."

They burst into laughter, then told me they did not need to question anyone else from our group.

After I came out, David and Patrick went in. A few moments later, the officers again exploded in laughter. The place was beginning to feel like a carnival. When Patrick came out, we asked him what had happened. He said that for nineteen years he had always sent flowers to his wife on their anniversary and asked the officers, "Let me at least call her and send her a kiss." That made us laugh, too. But then I remembered seeing him crying the night before when everyone else was asleep. I had not asked him about it, but maybe he had been thinking about his wife.

The officers finished the interrogations and left. Our group went back inside, swept the floors and settled in again. As some dozed off to sleep, I returned to writing in my diary.

The relative silence was broken when the guards started shouting, "Turkiya, Turkiya, Turkiya." We stood up again and started walking out of the shed, some of us cursing, others shaking our heads. It was yet another head count. As usual my name was mispronounced, as were a number of others. Turks from the other shed who were not part of our group were also called out and counted.

After the count, I saw the Pakistani doctor. I told him I had bad diarrhea and he gave some pills for it. He also wrote his name and personal data on a piece of paper and asked me to notify his embassy if we were released.

We went back into the shed. The heat was rising and there was a heavy smell in the air. Patrick, David, and Husnu were sitting together. Husnu had been listening to the 11 am news broadcasts and filled us in.

There was one report that it would take two months for the number of American troops in the Gulf to reach a quarter of a million, compared with a total of a hundred and seventy thousand Iraqi soldiers. French President Mitterand said that because Iraq had closed its borders French citizens could not leave and France therefore considered them to be prisoners. According to another report, citizens of Western countries were not allowed to leave Iraq. We wondered which category we fell into: Westerners or Easterners? A weary silence fell over us.

The guard who had brought us the fruit the other day came into the shed, looked over his shoulder to see he wasn't being followed and whispered, "You will meet your ambassador tomorrow."

We were not impressed by this. The Iraqis had proven to be adept at keeping us in limbo, giving us false hopes and stringing us along. At this point, there was no reason to believe anything they said.

After the guard left, some of the Turks from the other shed came by. They had been taken from Kuwait days after we had been abducted and said that Iraqis were looting homes. They also said that some Kuwaitis were protesting against the occupation.

At 2 pm, it was reported on the radio that a large group of Dutch nationals would be released by Iraq following an agreement reached with The Netherlands. The only news regarding Turkey was that the Indian foreign minister would be visiting - not exactly what we were hoping to hear. As always, we felt that the world was on one side, a homicidal lunatic was on the other and we were in the middle.

At 2:30 pm, an officer came with yet another list in his hand. With the translating assistance of the young Palestinian man who had created problems for us earlier, he read off the names of the thirty-two of us in the TJV group and then left.

A while later, some guards came and ordered Patrick to go with them. After Patrick had left, David became depressed. He didn't talk to anyone and stared down at the ground. I told our people to keep an eye on him. Eventually, he appeared to fall asleep.

Now it was being reported that France was going to contribute to the international coalition against Iraq and was expected to put together the second largest military force in the Gulf after the Americans. It would include fifty fighter aircraft and the aircraft carrier Clemenceau. Renewed concerns were reported about Iraq's chemical weapons capability. As usual, the news gave us the sense that all the powers were playing a game of brinkmanship and that we were just chips and pawns.

Then there was some news that really caught our attention, a report about nine Japanese being released by Iraq. We strongly hoped that Mr. Tanaka was among them and that he would give our names to the Turkish embassy in Baghdad. But by now we had learned to temper our expectations.

The young Palestinian man came around again to apologize. I accepted his apology and the subject was closed. He then said that he wanted to help us. He told us that he had to return to the hospital for medical treatment and that if we had dollars he could exchange them for Iraqi dinars. Now we were sure he was an informant. How else could he be coming and going in and out of the prison area without being escorted by guards?

For David it continued to be difficult with Patrick gone. He descended further into depression, going back over the events that led to his captivity, wondering what he might have done differently, whether he would ever get out. It was something that all of us went through, but it was really getting to him now. He kept saying that his secretary had wanted to change the date of his airline reservation for Kuwait. If he had only followed her suggestion, he wouldn't be here now. But he had not and now he was needlessly damning himself for it.

David was young, not more than thirty, with Chinese features. He was in good physical shape and seemed to be a very organized, diligent person. But now he seemed to be coming apart. We did our best to reassure him, but some in our group were having difficulty holding up as well, as the circumstances and the uncertainty continued to take their toll on all of us. Why was our embassy silent? Why was there nothing about us on the radio? Was the Turkish government working to get us released? Did they even know where we were?

All day long the guards had been abusing the Indian and Bangladeshi prisoners, shouting at them for no reason and pushing them around. I warned our group that the guards were getting increasingly edgy and told them to avoid confrontations.

At 6 pm it was reported that foreigners except for Americans and Western Europeans could leave Iraq through Jordan. That seemed to be encouraging. It was also reported that one of the Iraqi delegates attending the Arab summit in Cairo had walked

141

out.   For its part, Washington was saying that military intervention would not be a simple matter.

I went over to chat with David, hoping to give him a lift. He started telling me about himself and his family. He said that he had taken out a mortgage to buy an expensive home and was concerned that his wife could not manage to make the payments. "She is a housewife, she doesn't know about such things," he said.   There were also the bills for his daughter's schooling.

David said he had started out poor, working as a laborer. He said he had nearly died in a number of industrial accidents. Once, when there was a gas leak in a storage tank, he had collapsed and was unconscious for twenty minutes before he was rescued. Another time he was in a tank and the floor was flooded with water. A live electrical cord broke off and if it hadn't been for his new boots he would have been electrocuted.

By recounting these events, he seemed to be trying to give himself strength and hope that he could survive what he was going through now. I said to him that one way or another our situation had to be resolved relatively soon. He was still anxious, but after talking about his concerns his spirits seemed a little higher.

At 6:30 pm it was reported that Saddam Hussein had ordered business owners in Kuwait to re-open their enterprises by Saturday, August 11th, in other words, tomorrow. He said the government would not tolerate any failure to comply with his declaration.

I said, "Hey, guys, we have to be back on the job in Kuwait by tomorrow. If anyone does not show up, I will have to officially inform Saddam."

A while later, the guards turned on the television in the courtyard because Saddam Hussein was sending a message to the Arab summit. The Pakistani doctor helped translate for our group. Saddam called on the Arab world to join in a revolution to overthrow King Fahd of Saudi Arabia and President Mubarak of Egypt because they had helped the U.S. to deploy its military forces in the region. He also called on believers in Islam around the world to retaliate against Americans and American embassies if there were an attack on Iraq.

After listening to his diatribe, we hoped that one day God would give this utterly miserable man a normal brain and a regular state of mind.

After Saddam's speech, the guards began ordering the Bangladeshis into rows in the courtyard for a head count. There were at least two hundred of them. As always when the Bangladeshis were counted it turned into comedy that provided us with rare entertainment. The names were called individually and most of the Bangladeshi names began with Muhammad, for example, Muhammad Bin Abdulrahman, Muhammad Abdulrahman Bin Muhammad, Muhammad Bin Abdulrahman.

Whenever a name was called, at least four or five Bangladeshi would stand up and start arguing about whose name had been called. "He called my name, not yours," one would say. "No, that was my name!" another would say.

Today, the Bangladeshis seemed almost deliberately trying to confuse the guards, forcing them to start the count over a number of times. There had been a rumor that fifteen Bangladeshis had escaped and the guards seemed particularly determined to get the count right. Some of us wondered if the Bangladeshis were trying to cover for those who had escaped, but Mehmet Cetinkoprulu said that it was common for Bangladeshis to have similar names.

There was a report on the Iraqi television station that that had us roaring with laughter. During dinner at the summit meeting in Cairo, three of the Iraqi delegates had thrown plates at the foreign minister of the deposed Kuwaiti government, hitting him in the head and briefly knocking him unconscious. Doctors had been brought in to stitch his wounds. Even at the highest levels, the crisis was descending into slapstick. Some of us fell asleep grinning.

A little after 10 pm, we were jolted awake by guards again shouting, "Turkiya, Turkiya, Turkiya." Annoyed and groggy, we were in no mood for another head count.

"Gather up all your belongings; you are leaving," the guards said.

At this point we were really fed up. Refusing to stand, we said, "No, we're not going anywhere. Just count us here and be done with it."

The guards swore that we were really going to be released, and even mentioned the name of some hotel where we would be taken. The Pakistani doctor heard this and came running to give us his addresses in Pakistan and in Kuwait. One of the guards loaned us his pen to write down the information.

A few moments later we were being led out of the courtyard in a different direction, away from the flooded passageway, and into a single-story building. It was some sort of dormitory, with bunks and mattresses. Taner had always been complaining that the shed where we had been held was not like the prisons he had imagined or seen in the movies, so we said to him, "Congratulations, finally you have found the prison of your dreams."

Exhausted from only two hours sleep I lay down on one of the bunk beds. I had almost forgotten what it was like to stretch out on something other then concrete or sand. Still, the room was stifling hot, so some of my colleagues asked the guards if they could sleep outside on the walkway between the building and a nearby garden. The guards were stunned, asking why anyone would want to sleep on concrete when they were being offered a bed. They couldn't understand that we had actually become accustomed to sleeping on a hard surface. But it was true. Human beings can adapt to just about anything if they have to. And for some of us, sleeping on the ground was not really a problem if it meant cooler air.

Before going to sleep, we discovered that there were showers. We also noticed that soldiers were coming in and out to retrieve clothes and other article from the closets. We realized that we had been put in a barracks; the solders had been moved somewhere else to accommodate us.

On my way to the bathroom I could see a nearby building through the windows. The Chinese prisoners had been put in there. The space was larger but there were no bunk beds. I washed up briefly, too tired to take a shower. I went back to the bunk and slept soundly through the night.

Ali R. Bozkurt

Saturday, August 11th, 1990

I woke up to the sound of doves cooing outside the window. They were in a garden and the sight of green plants and shrubbery was never so beautiful.

Members of our group were showering and getting cleaned up for the first time in more than a week. Everyone seemed to have a renewed bounce in their step. Afterward, most of us lounged around on the grass by the garden.

An Iraqi soldier walked up and ordered everyone to go inside and sit on their bunks where, of course, we were again counted. This time we didn't mind so much because it seemed like we might actually be getting out. We were then led to the main square where we were seated in rows of five for another count.

A group of Iranians and Chinese were lined up there as well. There were two buses. The Iranians and the Chinese were placed on one and we were ordered to board the other. I looked around at the members of our group and could see that the anticipation was mounting in everyone. Hopes were up, but we had learned to expect anything in this game. Since we were being transported along with the Chinese and the Iranians, it was unlikely that we were being taken to our embassy. So, as far as we knew, it was just the beginning of another unknown journey.

We took our usual places on the bus. I sat in front while Mehmet Cetinkoprulu, who knew Baghdad, sat right behind me. Taner was in the next seat. For the first time, the military guard who rode on the bus with us was unarmed. Before leaving the barracks we had filled our barrel with water. We had not been given any food but water, as always, was the most important thing.

An escort car pulled away with its lights flashing but no siren. Our bus followed it out of the square toward the main road inside the base. The next part of the journey had begun. Maybe we would be released, or maybe we would be taken to a missile site or chemical weapons factory to be used as human shields. There was simply no way to know.

Taner, of course, predicted the worst: that we would be taken to southern Iraq and placed in front of invading American ground forces. He kept wringing his hands and asking if we could stop or asking the base commander if we could make just one telephone call to our homes and all kinds of other impossible things.

As we drove toward the exit, we passed a number of other sheds like the ones where we had been held. They too were crowded with prisoners. The road leading out of the base went up over a hill and we were able to look back with a bird's eye view. Indeed, it was a huge sprawling place, almost a metaphor for Iraq itself - one big military camp. It really was not a misnomer to call this country the Iraqi Military Union.

A few moments later and we were driving down tree-lined streets, a gentle breeze enhancing the coolness of the morning. Further on, we passed though date and orange groves, streaks of sunlight dancing through the branches of the trees and dazzling our eyes, gardens adorning the houses nestled in between the rows of fruit. Later we passed the kinds of arched gateways and walled squares that give Baghdad its air of magic, mystery and, at times, menace. I thought how much I would like to visit this city in other circumstances. I looked across from me and saw that Taner was still agitated. I said to him, "Look, just make believe that we're on a tourist bus enjoying all the beautiful sights."

After a while, it seemed we were traveling toward the center of the city. Stop lights became frequent and the streets more crowded with people. Life went on as usual in Baghdad, everyone busy with one thing and another, no-one noticing us as we passed.

At one stoplight, the guard exited the bus, left the door open behind him and walked around in front. It struck me that I could simply step out and blend right into the mass of pedestrians walking by. I even went so far as to move Taner's bag, which was in front of me, to the side. Taner immediately got suspicious and asked why I had moved it. I said that it was better that way.

The guard finished talking to his colleagues in the escort car and returned to the bus and we were moving again. As we approached the next intersection, Mehmet Cetinkoprulu said that down to the right was another prison camp, as well as a military base with missile installations. We all felt that now familiar sinking feeling, that sense that just when things might have been looking up, hell was around the corner. However, the bus turned to the left and Mehmet said to me, "Okay, Agbey," meaning big brother. "We're still in the clear."

We saw a hotel coming up on the left and our pulses quickened. But the bus kept on going down the road. A few moments later, however, our little caravan made a U-turn, and we could barely contain ourselves when our bus followed the escort car into the parking lot of the hotel. It seemed that our ordeal might finally be coming to an end.

The hotel, a fairly luxurious place, was on the Tigris River. I paid little attention to the name of it, as my mind was racing with thoughts of freedom and, at the same time, fears that it might still be another trick. In the lobby we were ordered to sit on the floor, along with the Chinese and the Iranians, to be counted. The Iraqi soldiers had difficulty pronouncing the names of the Chinese, as they had been written phonetically in Arabic. The Chinese themselves helped them to get it right and eventually everyone was accounted for.

We were asked if we had eaten breakfast and when we said no, we were taken into a dining room. There were about twenty tables and at each setting were two soft boiled eggs. Everyone joked to Osman that his order had finally been fulfilled.

Despite all this fancy treatment, we were still uneasy. After we finished eating, we sat and waited to see what would happen next. There were some dark jokes that this had been our last meal and now we would be chained to an Iraqi missile installation.

Through a window we saw what seemed to be a pickup truck from the Iranian embassy parked in front of the hotel. The Iranians were called from the dining room and a short while later we saw them drive off in the pickup. A soldier told us that the Turkish embassy was sending a vehicle for us. The anticipation was overwhelming.

At about noon, the Turkish representatives arrived, a small group of low-level bureaucrats. When they found out that most of us had left our passports in Kuwait, they said they would have to go back to the embassy and prepare travel documents. We should wait until they returned.

"No way!" we said. We demanded that we be taken immediately to the embassy, where we could wait just as easily for documents.

I said to the representatives, "You're not going anywhere without taking us."

"No," one of them said. "Remain here and we will come back for you later."

I told him, "Take us out of here immediately or I will rip the embassy up by its foundation and bury your ass beneath it!"

One of the representatives said, "We will have to speak with the commander here."

"In that case, I will go with you," I said.

We went together to the Iraqi officer in charge. He just waved his hands, signaling to the representatives from the embassy that we could leave right away.

I asked him, "May I speak with the commander in English?"

"Of course," he said. "Go ahead."

Before I could start, the Turkish representative said to me, "Why don't you stay here at the hotel tonight. We can find some other accommodation for workers who may not be able to afford it."

I said to him, "If you don't get ten taxies here immediately, I will turn your mouth and nose into a bloody mess."

He seemed to relent and asked, "Where can we find taxis?"

I asked the commander. He spoke with two soldiers who went out into the middle of road in front of the hotel, stopped two minibuses and ordered all the passengers off. They told the drivers to pick up our group at the hotel and that we would pay them. Soon after, we were on our way to the embassy.

When we arrived we found that Mr. Tanaka had indeed delivered to the embassy the list of names and data that Osman had written out for him to take. Until then, the embassy had had no idea we were imprisoned in Baghdad. Soon after we arrived, a list came from the Finnish embassy, provided by the Finnish prisoners we had cooperated with. We then did our part, giving all the lists of names of the various national groups we had to the Turkish ambassador. He would distribute them to the appropriate embassies so that they would know too about their still imprisoned citizens.

The next step was to wait for our travel documents to be prepared. Some of us went to a restaurant on the banks of Tigris and ordered the whitefish and raki we had been dreaming about since Basra.

On the way back we stopped at a grill to get some chicken for our colleagues who had remained at the embassy. As we waited for our order, it occurred to me that maybe we could find a way to fly to Amman rather than take another bus ride. I heard the owner of the grill speaking Turkish, so I asked him if I could use his telephone to call the airlines.

"No," he said. "I do not know the numbers of any airlines and it is not possible for you call anyone from here." I could tell he was suddenly very scared. Then he went over to his telephone and made a number of calls, all the while watching me with fear in his eyes.

Now I was becoming unsettled. We were finally free but we were still in Iraq, a country without justice or logic, and we could be arrested at any time for any reason. I noticed that there were pictures and photos of Saddam Hussein all over this establishment and remembered how it was said that one in every two Iraqis was an informer for the secret police. Saddam and his secret police were everywhere. Saddam Hussein was Iraq. No dictatorship could be as extreme as this one. And, despite our elation at being released from prison, being reminded that we were still in the middle of this country, where everyone was a prisoner, caused the fear to rise in us yet again.

Firmly, I said to the man, "Get off the phone!" He hesitated, then hung up, his hands trembling. So now we were scared of each other. We took ten of the fifteen chickens we had ordered and left immediately.

The embassy arranged for a bus to take us to Jordan. After a fifteen-hour overnight journey we arrived at the border and stopped at a gate where we had to go through immigration procedures.

When we got off the bus, European television crews and other media people descended upon us. We were among the first hostages released and they all wanted interviews. Some of us described the conditions in the camps where we had been held, then I started giving my views on Saddam Hussein. I said that he was like an actor in a one-man show and that as long as he remained in power, no-one would be able to deal rationally with Iraq. Before I could go any further, some of my colleagues grabbed me by the arms and started pulling me away, saying that we were not officially processed into Jordan yet and that the Iraqis could still detain us.

But I told them, no, it was over, and now I was going to do all I could as an individual to expose the nature of the Saddam Hussein dictatorship. So I kept talking, providing further details of our captivity, drawing a parallel between Saddam and Hitler, and saying that Saddam had to be held accountable for human rights violations before an international court of justice.

With the immigration process completed, we finally entered Jordan and were driven on to Amman. Finally, we were free from the grip of Saddam Hussein.

In Amman we were greeted by my good friends Mr. Abdul Kerim Hammad and Mr. Dabbas, Jordanian lawyers I had known for fifteen years. That night, we celebrated our freedom over dinner at a Lebanese restaurant, followed by a good sleep at a fine hotel.

Sunday, August 12th, 1990

When we woke up, it was still hard to believe that we were free. Jokingly, some of us asked which prison were we in now.

Around midday Mr. Abdul Kerim Hammad and his wife Leyla put on an enormous feast for us at their home. It had been so long since we had been able to enjoy the Arabic-style food that we had missed so much. We gorged ourselves on the thoroughly delicious meal, as if to take revenge against the starvation diet that had been imposed upon us.

Also invited to this gathering were a number of people, many of them lawyers, who also had been affected by the crisis or were following it very closely. Among them were an attorney from Saudi Arabia who had taken refuge in Jordan, some Kuwaitis and Jordanians of Egyptian descent who had fled Kuwait, and a number of Jordanians of Palestinian heritage, as well as numerous native Jordanians.

We engaged in a conversation that went on for many hours after the meal was over. It covered the entire situation in the region. Many points were made and many disputed. Still, it was generally agreed that the crisis in the Gulf was complex and rooted in many factors throughout the Middle East, and that unless the entire array of social, economic, political and geopolitical issues were adequately addressed, it would be difficult to achieve peace.

It seemed that the various views expressed at this gathering reflected the sentiment throughout much of the region. One statement by Abdul Kerim Hammad resonated with all of us: "Most Arabs are ruled by dictatorships of one kind or another. The dictators are surrounded by self-serving, obsequious people who treat the dictators as if they were divine, as if they were the receptacles of great wisdom and could do no wrong. I wish that it were a democratic Arab country calling for unity rather the regime of Saddam Hussein. It would be truly meaningful and our voices would be so much stronger if Arab nations could peacefully and democratically unite and cooperate with each other in the pursuit of common goals and interests."

During the discussion a number of factors were viewed as contributing to the ongoing crisis. One was discrimination within the Arab world. Saudi Arabia, for example, had been utilizing labor from Egypt and Yemen and paying those workers $50 per month. At the same time, the Saudis were paying their own office boys $1,000 per month. Weren't they all Arabs? Why should there be such a huge disparity?

Another view was that the Saudi and Kuwaiti emirs were keeping the oil wealth for themselves, while allowing the British to exploit Kuwait and America to exploit Saudi Arabia. Those portrayed in the media as Arab leaders had little or no connection with the vast majority of Arab people they claimed to represent. The so-called Arab leaders were transferring control of the oil to America and Britain solely for the benefit of themselves and their families.

There was also the question of imbalanced treatment and hypocrisy. A number of people said that far more noise was being made about Iraq at the United Nations than about the deaths of Palestinian children. Others emphasized that Jordanian King Hussein's popular support had doubled to nearly one hundred percent since he had stood up to Saddam Hussein. Further evidence of the King's effort to connect with ordinary citizens was his statement that he no longer wanted to be addressed as "Your Majesty."

Surveying the region, it was noted that twenty-three Arab nations were ruled by dictatorships. Jordan was the single country enjoying even a partial democracy, and that had been true for only ten months. Ironically, now that Jordan was more democratic and the King was seeking to be more representative of the views of Jordanian citizens, the King was the target of criticism by the U.S.

The discussion returned to comparisons between Kuwait and Palestine. The view was expressed that the Kuwaitis had surrendered to Iraq without hardly firing a shot. Yet even Palestinian children defended themselves against the powerful Israeli military by throwing stones and were ready to die for their cause. If you sent a kilo of sugar to someone in Palestine, he would use only what he needed and share the rest with his neighbors. How come such a fuss was being made over the Kuwaitis, who did not even have the courage to fight back?

Most of the time I was listening rather than speaking. Whenever someone mentioned the idea of Arab nationalism or Arab union, I was tempted to say that achieving Arab unity would be nearly impossible, that it might be easier to unify all the Turkic peoples spread across Asia.

Eventually I did comment, saying that we had all lived under the Ottoman Empire for five hundred years. As Muslims, we had been united. But many things had gotten in the way and we had become divided. Today, Arabs were killing one another even though they were all Muslims. That meant that the problem ran deeper than just questions of religion or nationalism.   If there was to be any type of unity and real cooperation in the region, there had to be a mutual understanding of the priorities of each nation in the region, as expressed democratically through the will of their citizens.

During the discussion, the Jordanians and Palestinians tended to agree that Saddam Hussein represented Arab nationalism, but that he was a dictator and his methods were wrong. They agreed with Saddam's position that Israel should withdraw from Palestine, Syria from Lebanon and America from Saudi Arabia before Iraq withdrew from Kuwait. They said they wished he were not a dictator, because then he could be more effective in the cause. But if he was willing to die for Arab independence then they were too.

The focus turned to Pakistan, with people saying the U.S. had undermined the government of Prime Minister Benazir Bhutto because she had refused to cooperate against Iraq. There were thousands of Pakistani soldiers working in Saudi Arabia and the U.S. wanted Pakistan to contribute them to the military buildup. But Prime Minister Bhutto had declined. She was not like her predecessor, General Zia ul-Haq, who had been a puppet of America.   In retaliation, the U.S. had orchestrated the dismissal of her government only six days earlier.

Another issue was Iran, with the belief expressed that if Iraq was attacked and defeated then Iran would begin to expand into Arab nations. People seemed to be equating the fall of Saddam with increased threats to the Arab world, believing that the death of Saddam would lead only to more Arab deaths.

Some held the view that the economic pressure and the threat of attacks against Iraq would create a million versions of Carlos in the Arab world, that if Saddam were deposed, there would be biological and chemical attacks against New York. Some said that because Israel was killing Palestinian women and children with the permission of America, people felt they had nothing to lose.

Someone said that Iraq might have nuclear capability, that Saddam might actually be able to withstand a U.S. attack. Others noted that Israel was so concerned by the possibility of nuclear retaliation by Saddam that it was asking German firms exactly what types of devices and materials they had sold to Iraq.

An Iranian expressed his view of Israel, saying, "Europe created a Frankenstein and now this Frankenstein is devouring Europe." He noted what Mussolini had said in 1942 about the Jews: "Let them go ahead and establish their state, that way we will know where our enemies are."

One of the Jordanians said, "In this country, everyone believes that Israel is synonymous with America. We do not believe that Israel and America would protect the grave of Muhammad and we do not believe that America would leave when Saudi Arabia asked." The U.S. was therefore using Iraq as a pretext to cement its military presence in Saudi Arabia.

Another view was that while Europe was trying to establish a union, European nations were trying to keep the Arab world divided. If Europe could unite, than why couldn't the Islamic world come together as well?

The views we were hearing added up to perspective similar to what we had developed from following the news on our radio in prison - at least in the sense that the world's powerful nations were circling the Middle East like vultures, exploiting the region's oil reserves and protecting their own interests, to the detriment of the people of the region.

Finally the discussions ended and the gathering broke up. It was great to be with such stimulating friends and soon I would be reunited with my wonderful family and waking up at home in my own bed.

Still, I continued to go over in my mind all these complicated, overlapping issues and I knew that it would be some time before I would be able to fully digest the ten days we had just lived through. It had been a difficult and often painful journey, but one of enormous value, a unique experience for learning about ourselves, about others, and about the workings of the world. At the same time, it had endowed me with a mission: to work on behalf of civilians caught in the crossfire of war and to ensure that their rights were fully recognized in law and respected in practice, a truly necessary step if humanity was to continue moving forward. I believe that God put me through this experience so that I could carry out that mission.

As our group continued to be inundated by members of the media wanting to report on our story, I wrote a series of comments for distribution:

"Colonies attain the status of independent states when the rights of individual citizens are fully defined and guaranteed. In the world today, there are systems that enshrine and protect the sovereign rights of states. But the world has fallen short because there is no system with sufficient guarantees for individuals.

"Nations are able to come to the defense of a nation under attack, for example, Kuwait, and apply sanctions and other pressures against the aggressor nation, Iraq. But why is the world not able to mount sufficient pressure to protect the rights of individuals? That can happen only when the countries of the world agree to stand together to protect all people everywhere against repression and terror. That is the only way toward a world free from fear.

"Individual nations have used their courts to prosecute citizens of other nations. The Nuremberg trials and the prosecution of former Panamanian leader, Manuel Noriega, are examples. But unlike at Nuremberg, there was not an international consensus for the prosecution of Noriega and it did little or nothing to further the cause of respect for universal values. The Noriega case, in fact, only underlined the lack of acceptance in the world for unilateral actions by powerful countries.

"We would consider it a success if our efforts to hold Saddam Hussein legally accountable for his treatment of civilians moved the world closer to establishing a world judicial system in which individuals could seek redress for crimes committed against them by states. In the name of all the hostages who have been held or are still being held by Saddam Hussein, I therefore invite the leaders of every nation to work together to build such a system and to commit their nations to accepting and implementing the decisions of a world court once it is in operation.

"In taking up the case against Saddam Hussein, I think of those of us who are fortunate enough to have been freed and all those who are still being held against their will. I bow with respect to the memory of the moment in prison when as a group, hundreds of us, representing dozens of nations, decided that if we were released we would demand justice for the time we had been kept in utterly inhumane conditions, our lives reduced to bargaining chips in the hands of a megalomaniac. We decided then to fight for our rights as world citizens. Now, I feel the joy of moving forward with our decision. For those of you still imprisoned, I want you to know that the pain you are enduring will not be in vain if we can use our experience to ensure the strengthening of civilization for the betterment of humanity.

"I also think of the Iraqi soldiers who were part of our odyssey. I will not forget the horrible conditions that you must endure under the thumb of Saddam Hussein. And I recognize that although you were our jailers, for the most part we were treated in a decent, sometimes even courteous, manner. I therefore believe that you do not support the dictatorial ways of Saddam Hussein and that one day you will have the opportunity to live freely and democratically. So do not lose hope. May we all trust in God and may God help people everywhere, of every nationality, for we are all citizens of the world."

Ali R. Bozkurt

PLEASE GIVE THIS MESSAGE TO THE NEAREST TURKISH EMBASSY :)

Türk Elçiliğinin Dikkatine : Bizler Aşağıda isimleri bulunan şahıslar Bağdatta bir esir kampında bulunuyoruz. (Iraqi Military Police) En kısa zamanda hayatta olduğumuzu ailelerimize bildirmenizi ve kötü hayat şartları nedeniyle bir an önce kurtarılmamızı istiyoruz.

1. Ali Rıza Bınkurt (Ankara 136 21 28) Telefonlar
   (Firma Sahibi) Mühendis
2. Osman Mimaroğlu (ankara 213 6494)
   Proje Müdürü Mühendis
3. Mehmet Getakipoğlu (Ankara 213 8676)
   Proje Md. yrd. Mühendis
4. Sedat Yıldırım (İstanbul 360 75 19)
   (Kamp amiri)
5. Ömer Özkan Çiftçi
6. İbrahim
7. Hüsnü
8. Ahmet N.
9. Duran Baran
10. Taner Papila
11. Salman Sever (9-7721-2024)
12. Mehmet Gümüştaş (Dağbaşı nahiyesi
    Subarbaşı köyü Araklı Trabzon)
13. Ahmet Şahin (9-8793-1434)
14. Menderes Şahin (aynı)
15. Ali Kemal Bilaloğlu (Cumhuriyet
    mahallesi Üst Geçit Sarmaşık
    Sokak nö 17 Pamukova)
16. Mehmet Turgut ⎤
17. İbrahim Turgut ⎦ Sarıoğlan Palas
R. Ali Turgut   kasabası
19. Yusuf Turgut   Kayseri
20. Mehmet Turgut

21. Beytullah Yüksel 9-4761-1693
22. Hasan Zmirkıran 9.—
23. Cemil Y.

...oğlu (9-0291-1660)
... Yusuf Polat (9-388-17417)
29. Mehmet Gelebi (Karadeniz Gözbi 22 645)
30. Mehmet Kılıç (Göl bahkalıyesi Tepecik köyü
    B.Çekmece İstanbul.
31. Sıyami Dadaş (Sosa evler 27/20 Karabük
    Zonguldak)
32. Ali Köymen (7100 Sokak 15 34
    Organize Nafız Gürman mah.
    Karşıyaka İzmir)
33. Yaşar Koca
34. Mehmet Aşıkbaş   Toylıoaldıoğlu
35. Serbay Dikici
36. Eyüp Kadir Tartar
37. İbrahim Uslupehlivan
38. Mahmut Çağlar
39. Nurettin Çağlar
40. Ahmet Suğdüş
41. Bayram Pehlivan
42. Süleyman Kazanç
43. Uğur Kumaş

Yukarıdaki elemanlar Kuveytte İş yapan Turkish Joint Venture inşaat şirketinin elemanları ve Jahra Belediyesi Şoförleridir. Kuveytte esir ve Belediye elemanları ve Jahra Belediyesi Şoförleridr. Kuveytte esir edilerek getirilmişlerdir.

Ali R. Bozkurt

8.8.1990

Your excellency,

We've been brought to Baghdad as hostages, taken from our work with a Turkish construction company in Kuwait. We did not hear anything about us on the radio up to this day. Germans and British who were brought here with same condition as ours have been released. We believe that you'll be trying every possible way to get us released and that our government has such powers to demand our immediate freedom.

Sincerely
43 Turkish hostages

43 Turkish hostages, under very difficult conditions, soaking in urine and feces are fighting for survival. Our only strength is God.

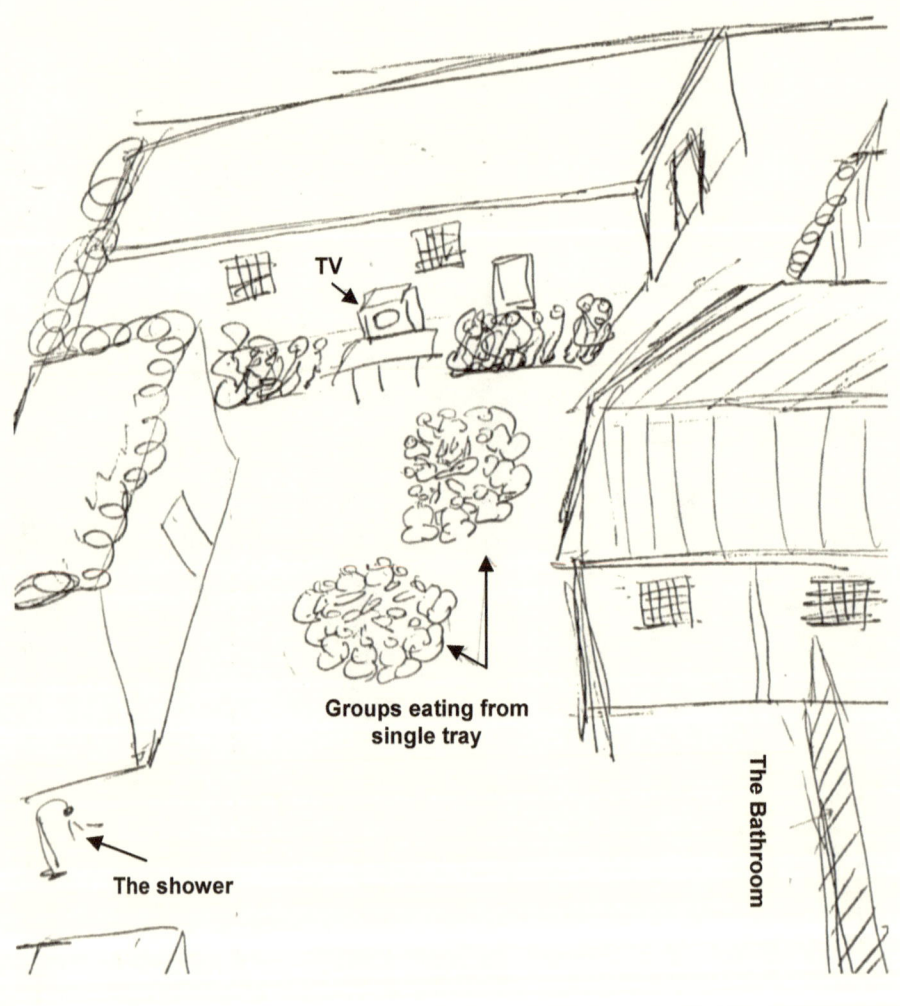

TV

Groups eating from
single tray

The Bathroom

The shower

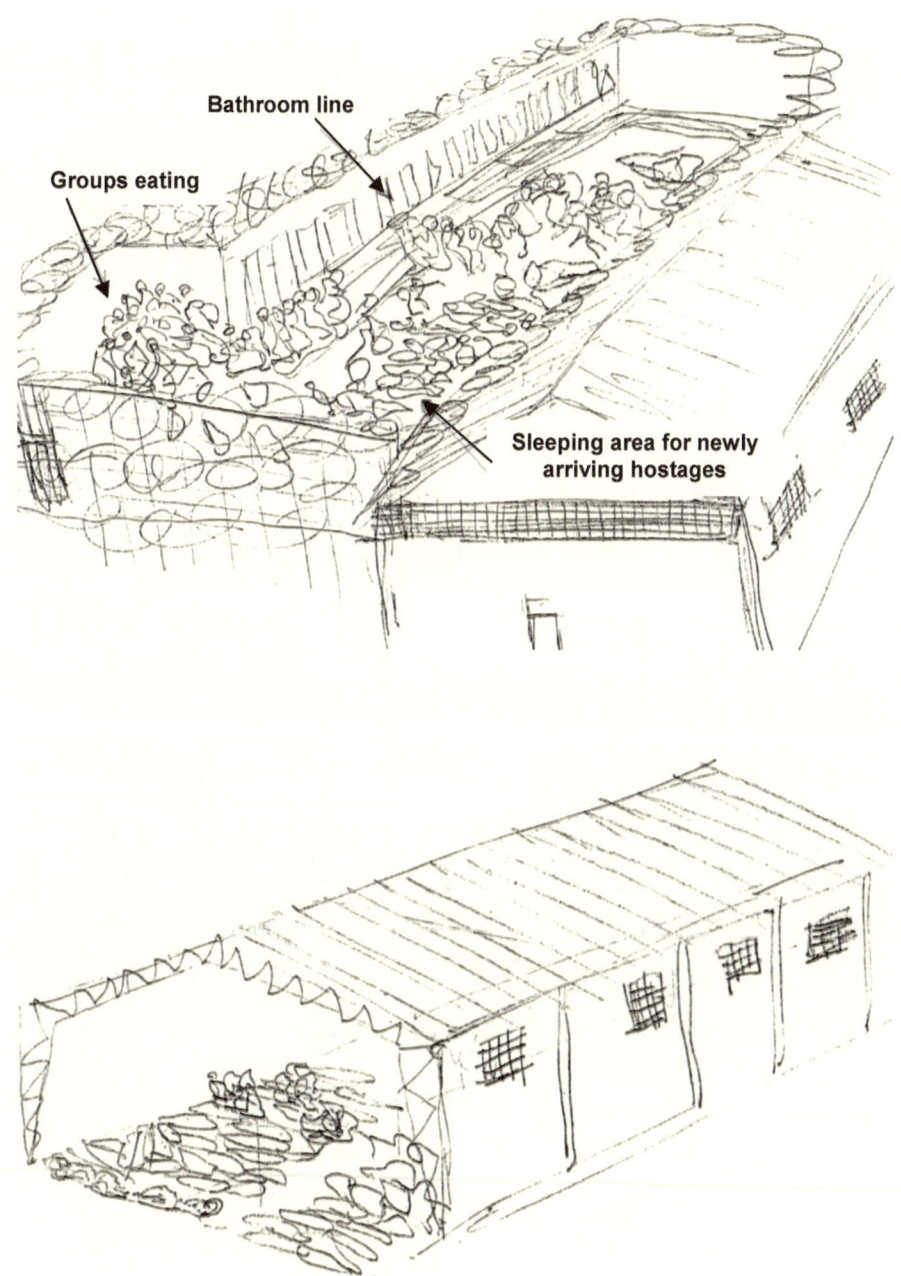

167

Inside the prison - people sleeping on the ground.

Cafeteria
Restaurant

TJV Labour Camp

Ali R. Bozkurt

"Bizi, savaş esiri diye caddelerde gezdirdiler"

Kuveyt'te 2 Ağustos günü İrak askerlerince gözaltına alınan 53 Türk'ten Türk şirketi TVJ'nin Yönetim Ku
rulu Başkanı Ali Rıza Bozkurt 11 günlük serüvenden sonra Esenboğa'da eşi ve çocuklarıyla sevgi yumağ
oluşturdu. Bozkurt "Bizi önce Basra'ya sonra Bağdat'a götürdüler. Bizi 'Savaş esirleri' diye caddelerde
dolaştırırken yüzbinlerce gösterici 'Savaşı kazandık' şeklinde slogan atıyordu" dedi (Yazısı 7. sayfada

About the Author

Graduated from Istanbul technical university in 1963, Ali's construction company specialized in road building, airports, tunnels and power plants.

Following his hostage ordeal, he immersed himself in political, social justice, human rights and constitutional law issues, becoming an election observer for the National Endowment for Democracy in several newly-independent states and an international business advisor to the New Jersey legislature.

As a Research Fellow at Harvard University's Kennedy School of Government in the late 1990s, Ali undertook a several years long study of constitutional law, state and religion conflicts and political party organization.

He has over twenty books published following his release from Saddam.